1.50

JOYCE CHEN
COOK BOOK

JOYCE CHEN COOK BOOK

BY JOYCE CHEN

FOREWORD BY PAUL DUDLEY WHITE, M.D.

BARNES & NOBLE BOOKS
A DIVISION OF HARPER & ROW, PUBLISHERS
New York, Cambridge, Philadelphia, San Francisco
London, Mexico City, São Paulo, Sydney

A hardcover edition of this book was published by J.B. Lippincott Company.

JOYCE CHEN COOK BOOK.Copyright © 1962 by Joyce Chen. All rights reserved. Printed in the United States of America. No part of this book may be used or reproduced in any manner whatsoever without written permission except in the case of brief quotations embodied in critical articles and reviews. For information address Harper & Row, Publishers, Inc., 10 East 53rd Street, New York, N.Y. 10022. Published simultaneously in Canada by Fitzhenry & Whiteside Limited, Toronto.

First BARNES & NOBLE BOOKS edition published 1983.

LIBRARY OF CONGRESS CATALOGUE CARD NUMBER: 82-49008

ISBN: 0-06-464060-4 (previously ISBN: 0-397-00285-8)

83 84 85 86 10 9 8 7 6 5 4 3 2

Contents

It is best to use a ruler or paper as a guide when checking this table to be sure of not looking at the wrong line.

It is best to use a ruler or paper as a guide when checking this table to be sure of not looking at the wrong line.

Dish	Page no.	Inexpensive	Moderate	Expensive	Short Preparation	Moderate Preparation	Long Preparation	Short Cooking	Moderate Cooking	Long Cooking	Steaming	Serve Immediately	Serve Hot	Serve Cold (Cook ahead)	Can be reheated	Reheating-not recommended	Cannot be reheated	Main dish	2nd Main dish	Vegetable dish	Salad	Hors d'oeuvres	Snacks	Children's dish	Light flavored dish	Moderate flavored dish	Heavy flavored dish	Hot spicy flavored dish	Emergency dish (quick and easy)	Dessert	Afternoon snack
Beef With Green Beans (String Beans)	120		•		•			•				•		•	•			•						•		•					
Beef With Mushrooms	121		•		•		•						•		•			•								•					
Chungking Beef Shreds — Hot	122	•				•		•				•			•			•										•			
Spiced Beef With Soy Sauce	123	•		•					•				•	•	•			•									•				
Jellied Lamb Loaf	124	•		•					•				•			•		•													
Pork:	126																														
Pork With Bean Sprouts	128	•			•							•						•								•					
Mandarin Moo Shi Pork (With Pancakes)	129		•		•				•				•					•								•					
Pork With Bean Thread (Chinese Vermicelli)	130		•						•				•					•								•					
Pork Chops, Shanghai Style	131		•		•			•				•		•				•									•				
Chungking Pork	132		•		•			•				•		•				•										•			
Pork With Green Peas	133	•			•			•				•						•						•	•						
Mandarin Sweet And Sour Pork	134		•					•				•			•									•		•					
Shanghai Ham	135		•		•					•		•						•								•					
Lion Head	136		•				•			•		•						•								•					
Stuffed Cucumbers	138	•			•			•				•						•						•		•					
Steamed Meat Cake	140		•		•						•	•						•								•					
Seafood:	141																														
Fried Shrimp — Chinese Style	146		•	•	•			•				•			•			•						•							
Shrimp With Green Peas	147		•	•	•			•				•			•			•							•						
Shrimp With Black Beans	148		•	•	•			•				•			•			•								•					
Sweet And Sour Shrimp	149		•	•					•			•			•			•						•		•					
Shrimp With Lobster Sauce	150		•	•					•			•			•			•						•		•					
Lobster In Meat Sauce	151		•	•					•			•			•			•						•		•					
Soy Sauce Fish — Shanghai Style	152	•		•					•				•			•	•									•					
Steamed Fish	154	•		•				•			•	•					•	•						•							
West Lake Sweet And Sour Fish (Especially For Fishermen)	155	•			•		•					•						•						•		•					
Eggs:	157																														
Mandarin Eggs	159	•		•			•					•			•			•						•							
Crab Meat With Eggs	160	•		•	•			•				•			•			•						•		•					•
Folded Fried Eggs In Soy Sauce	161	•		•			•					•			•			•						•							•
Egg Foo Yung	162		•	•				•				•						•						•		•					
Egg Garnish	164	•		•			•						•				•							•							

Chart guide for vegetable, fried rice, noodle, and dessert recipes. The vertical note at the right side of the chart reads:

It is best to use a ruler or paper as a guide when checking this table to be sure of not looking at the wrong line.

Recipe	Page no.	Inexpensive	Moderate	Expensive	Short Preparation	Moderate Preparation	Long Preparation	Short Cooking	Moderate Cooking	Long Cooking	Steaming	Serve Immediately	Serve Hot	Serve Cold (Cook ahead)	Can be reheated	Reheating not recommended	Cannot be reheated	Main dish	2nd Main dish	Vegetable dish	Salad	Hors d'oeuvres	Snacks	Children's dish	Light flavored dish	Moderate flavored dish	Heavy flavored dish	Hot spicy flavored dish	Emergency dish (quick and easy)	Dessert	Afternoon snack
Vegetables:	165																														
Cucumber Salad With Chicken Shreds	167		●		●				●					●						●						●					
Peking Spinach Salad With Mustard Dressing	168	●			●			●						●						●							●				
Chinese Cabbage With Chicken Fat	169	●			●				●					●						●				●							
Sweet And Sour Cabbage Relish (Can Be Hot)	170	●			●			●							●					●							●	●			
Sweet And Sour Radish Salad	171	●													●		●			●							●				
Bean Sprouts Salad With Egg Garnish	172	●				●								●	●					●		●		●							
Spinach — Chinese Style	173	●			●			●				●		●						●					●						
Mushrooms With Bean Curd	174		●		●			●					●		●					●					●						
Asparagus Salad	175	●			●			●					●	●						●					●						
Green Beans	175	●			●			●					●							●						●	●				
Celery Salad	176	●			●									●	●					●							●				
Cauliflower	177	●			●			●						●	●					●											
Mushrooms, Bamboo Shoots And Pea Pods	178		●		●				●			●			●					●					●						
Fried Rice:	179																														
Egg Fried Rice — Family Style	180	●			●				●				●					●						●	●						
Fried Rice — Cantonese Style	181	●			●				●									●						●	●						
Choo Choo Train Fried Rice	182	●				●								●										●	●						
Chinese Noodles:	183																														
Peking Meat Sauce Noodles	184	●				●		●				●					●							●		●					●
Chinese Fried Noodles: Both Sides Golden	187		●			●		●				●		●				●	●					●							●
Soft Fried	188	●				●		●				●						●	●					●	●						●
Chinese Noodles In Soup	190	●				●						●						●						●							●
Dessert:	192																														
Almond Float	193	●			●									●																●	●
Almond Tea	194	●				●	●					●		●																●	●
Orange Tapioca — Chinese Style	196	●			●							●		●																●	●
Steamed Egg Cake	196	●			●				●			●		●																●	●
Pea Jelly Square	198	●			●			●					●																	●	

Foreword

Joyce chen's recipes are commendable for several reasons. In the first place, they are a delight to the gourmet; secondly, they represent real Chinese cooking at its best; and thirdly, they are good for the health.

Many of us physicians are interested in the need of prescribing food which has a favorable effect not only on the taste buds, but also on the walls of the arteries, inasmuch as atherosclerosis (rusting of the arteries) is undoubtedly increased by overnutrition, which is as dangerous in this country in these days as undernutrition was at the time of the Pilgrim Fathers, and still is in many parts of the world.

The skillful and interesting use of vegetable dishes with sauces that are not over rich, and of meats and fish which are moderate in their fat content, combine to supply a diet which can be heartily recommended, provided the calories are kept at a reasonable level for the overnourished citizens of the western world.

These comments of mine are based not only on scientific fact but also on personal experience at Joyce Chen's restaurant where our family has enjoyed on many occasions Joyce Chen's delightful cuisine.

Paul Dudley White, M.D.

Preface

DURING THE TIME THAT I WAS IN CHINA I HAD THE PRIVI-
lege of sampling the best Chinese cuisine in many homes and
famous restaurants and was so fascinated by the wonders of this
ancient art that I even learned to do some of the simpler dishes
under the watchful but amused eyes of several excellent Chinese
chefs. When I came home, a search for restaurants offering a
similar level of Chinese cooking proved so fruitless that I was
forced to try to cook Chinese dishes for myself.

For help I turned to the many books which have been
printed on Chinese cooking, read them all, and tried out recipes
from most, with varying success. Not one of these books was really
satisfactory. Some had been so "adapted to American kitchens,
grocery stores, and tastes" that the dishes they describe are not
really Chinese at all. Others assumed that an American cook
knew procedures and methods that are simple enough, but were
taken for granted by a Chinese chef. Quite a few of these books
were written by Chinese to be sure, but by people who never
cooked in China or obviously had no experience of Chinese cooking at its best. Worst of all were the collections of recipes clearly
taken from other cookbooks and not even tested for accuracy by
the author in person. Some of these recipes, even when carefully
followed, came out to incredible, inedible, and unattractive
dishes which would horrify even a Chinese coolie.

Bit by bit I stumbled into fairly passable Chinese cooking for myself, but I felt sorry for the people who would think that Chinese cooking is what is described in these books and would be discouraged by lack of adequate directions to prepare the simple Chinese dishes, to say nothing of the very complex delights inadequately described in some of these books.

Only a few Chinese restaurants in the United States offer Cantonese, Shanghai, Peking and other dishes prepared by really first-class Chinese chefs. But what is the gourmet interested in exploring one of the world's great cuisines to do if he does not live near one of these restaurants? Having sampled the joys of Joyce Chen's Restaurant in Cambridge, you can imagine how happy I was to learn that she was writing a Chinese cookbook based on her own knowledge and personal experience of the finest cooking in China and on the results of teaching in her classes the simple ways to get equally good results in an American kitchen. So here is her book — one which will start you out on the right road to fine Chinese cooking. All you have to do is to follow *exactly* her directions and you cannot fail to prepare for yourself an authentic, attractive and delightful Chinese meal. When you have then made a good beginning, she has promised a more advanced book which will make you qualified to cook for a mandarin if not for an emperor.

ROBERT S. WOODBURY

Dedication

THIS BOOK IS DEDICATED TO MY PARENTS, MR. AND Mrs. Hsin-shih Liao who led me to share their interest and knowledge of Chinese cookery.

For several generations my family had worked with government. My grandfather was a governor and two of his brothers were of the cabinet rank in the late Chin Dynasty. My father, for many years had been a railroad administrator and city executive. He was decorated for his distinguished service in relief work for the famine-stricken victims.

In old-time China high ranking government officials used to employ a number of servants and housemaids. Their children did not need to do any housekeeping. But my family was one of the rare exceptions. When I was a young girl, my parents always encouraged me to stand on my own feet. They trained me to do things myself. Whenever I entered the kitchen, my mother never forgot to remind me that I should learn how to cook so I wouldn't eat rice raw in case I couldn't afford a family cook in the future.

Nearly thirty years have elapsed since my parents' death. I have appreciated and treasured their influence and training all the time. The publication of this book is to express my indebtedness to them.

How I Came To Write This Book

WHEN I WAS A YOUNG GIRL IN PEKING, WHERE I was born, the most interesting thing to me was making miniature pastries for myself while our family chef was making others. My father was fond of good food. For a good wife like my mother the most important job was serving the best dishes to satisfy his appetite at every meal. For this reason we had a very excellent family chef whose dishes were not only good to eat but were also pretty and neat looking. My father entertained friends more frequently at home than in restaurants, by their enthusiastic request. Of my childhood all I remember are parties, guests and foods.

When my father's best friend, Uncle Li, became Ambassador to Russia he begged my father to let him have our chef to cook for him. Uncle Li knew that this would make life better for him in a strange land. After our chef left, my mother just could not find anyone to replace him. So my mother cooked for my father herself. My governess, who was the chef's wife, was the helper. I was often the watcher.

When I was eighteen I once cooked a banquet for a party. Cooking was such fun in China because the maids did all the washing and cutting. All I did was give the orders and cook. That party turned out to be a success which encouraged me to do more cooking and to study more about food. Frequently I

1

tried to figure out and to cook those dishes which were served in famous restaurants.

In April 1949 I came with my family to Cambridge, Massachusetts, from Shanghai, China. Very soon after that we invited a good many Chinese students at Harvard, M.I.T. and Boston University to dinner at our home. It is a traditional Chinese custom to urge friends to stay and eat. I enjoyed cooking for them, though it meant extra work for me, as I did not have a maid. I had my reward in seeing their pleased faces and hearing their appreciative comments. I made them feel at home, and they made me feel the same in this new country.

I still remember clearly the time I first made egg rolls for the Buckingham School bazaar. I made two dozen egg rolls and a few dozen cookies for the mothers' food table. When my daughter Helen came home from school I asked her, *Did you see my egg rolls there?* She replied, *No, I only saw your cookies there, not your egg rolls.* I thought they did not like them so they had not put them up for sale. But on the same evening when I was shopping I met one of the mothers who was in charge of the food table. She asked me, *Mrs. Chen, do you think you could make some more egg rolls, your egg rolls sold out in five minutes.* What a surprise to me. They did like them. I made dozens more the same night for that school.

Many American friends asked me once and again about Chinese cooking. They had tried recipes from different Chinese cookbooks and they all seemed to have confronted the same troubles. It was too hard to get the ingredients. The recipes were too complicated to follow and took too much time to prepare. Many dishes simply did not come out right.

This situation encouraged me greatly to conduct a cooking class for those friends who were interested in Chinese cooking. I donated the tuition from this class to the school scholarship fund. I have enjoyed their long-lasting friendship from then on.

2

Since I have come to know this country better I have realized that there is a large group of people who like authentic Chinese food, especially those who have visited or lived in China. All this time I had a desire to open a Chinese restaurant which would make American customers happy and Chinese customers proud. By the end of May 1958 we opened the Joyce Chen Restaurant in Cambridge.

I hope our restaurant is not only a place to enjoy truly authentic Chinese food, but may also serve as a cultural exchange center. I have the honor of being an American citizen and share the freedom and opportunity this country offers. In return I would like all Americans to enjoy my service.

In the fall of 1960 I started to teach Chinese cooking both at the Cambridge and the Boston Adult Education Centers. I was amazed to hear that there was a long waiting list of people who were interested in my classes.

The more people I know, the more I felt it was necessary to write a cookbook of my own which will offer my knowledge to the public. My book gives the basic and essential knowledge of Chinese cookery, recipes of Mandarin, Shanghai, Chunking and Cantonese origin. I do not wish to give you too many recipes in one book to confuse and discourage you. I only give you enough recipes which are easy to prepare to delight your family and your guests.

All recipes have been tested by hundreds of Americans. I simplified the procedure and still kept the authentic flavor. Photos and sketches will give you clear directions for practice.

From my heart I sincerely hope you will all use and enjoy this book. If you like it I will write a second one to offer you the more complicated dishes which we prepare in the advanced and gourmet classes.

Have a good time with your Chinese cooking.

JOYCE CHEN

3

CHINESE CABBAGE

BLACK BEANS

DRIED SHRIMP

CHINESE PEPPERCORNS

STAR ANISE

WINTER MELON

BAMBOO SHOOTS

BEAN CURD

BEAN SPROUT

GINGER ROOT

GOLDEN NEEDLES

BEAN THREAD

WATER CHESTNUTS

WOOD EAR

BLACK MUSHROOMS (DRIED)

SNOW PEAS

photo: Voss Greenough

Chinese Ingredients

THE INCONVENIENCE OF GETTING CHINESE INGRE-
dients discourages many people from cooking
Chinese dishes. Most big cities of the United
States have Chinatowns or Chinese groceries where
the needed ingredients can be obtained, but very
often beginners get the wrong items. To make your Chinese
cooking successful, the right ingredients are indispensable.

In this book I will tell you what to look for and show you
pictures of the Chinese ingredients which you are not familiar
with. Then at the end of the book you will find a list of these
ingredients specially arranged so you can tear it off and take it
with you to Chinatown.

If you recognize from my description and pictures what you
want, just point it out to a clerk *I want some of that.* If no such
things are in sight in the store, point out the items on your Chinese
shopping list and ask the clerk. Do not be afraid to tell the clerk
what you want it for; he may be able to help you.

If you still can not get what you want or if you live too far
away from a Chinatown, please do not hesitate to consult me at
this address: MRS. JOYCE CHEN, P.O. BOX 3, CAMBRIDGE, MASS.
02138. I shall be very glad to get it for you from my mail-
order department. Also write me if you have any trouble with
my recipes, but just make sure that you have done exactly the
way the recipes recommend.

There are many Chinese ingredients which sound and look strange to Americans. I only list those which are used in the recipes of this book. They are imported from Taiwan (Formosa), Hong Kong or Japan. Many are dried or canned. A few Chinese farms in New Jersey grow Chinese vegetables. More are scattered in Florida and California.

CHINESE CABBAGE

The kind of Chinese cabbage obtainable in super markets originally came from Northern China and is also named celery cabbage. I call this Chinese celery cabbage in my recipes. The white and firm cabbage is the best and good for cooking, stewing, or serving raw as salad.

Another kind of Chinese cabbage which is obtainable the year round in Chinese groceries has a white stalk with green leaves. It is good for cooking and stewing but cannot be eaten raw. The firm, shorter, and unflowered cabbages are fresh and tender.

CHINESE PEA PODS
(Snow Pea)

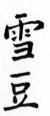

Chinese pea pods are also called snow peas. The plant looks exactly like regular peas, but inside the peas grow slowly, and the large pods are tender and crisp to eat. In preparing, snap off the ends and strings on both sides like green beans. Chinese cabbage and snow peas are sold in Chinatown groceries all year round. The price of Chinese cabbage is quite steady. Snow peas vary in price almost every day; in New England they range from 60 cents to four dollars per pound, depending on method of shipment, but you do not need very many at one time.

One day a customer phoned me to say that he had bought some peas in a supermarket to cook with beef and the pods were so tough that he could not chew them. Peas in American markets and snow peas in Chinese groceries are entirely different.

I once cooked some freshly picked sugar peas at my friend's

6

farm. I discovered they are different from Chinese snow peas. Sugar peas have reddish purple flowers; Chinese snow peas have white flowers and the pods are more crispy. Recently the frozen snow peas imported from Japan became available in certain stores. They are not so crisp and are smaller. I suspect they are of the kind of sugar peas with red flowers. Better buy fresh ones in Chinatown if you can. Snow peas in a plastic bag can be kept in the refrigerator for more than a week.

Since trade stopped with Red China, black mushrooms are all shipped in from Japan. They come dried. To prepare, pour boiling water over them, then let them soak in a covered bowl for 15 minutes or more. When the mushrooms turn soft, cut off stems, squeeze out the water and they are ready to use (the water may be used to replace water or stock in recipes if you like the strong flavor of black mushrooms). Dried black mushrooms may be kept in a cool and dry place for a long period; otherwise they might be wormeaten.

There are two varieties of black mushrooms. The one with a dark black surface is thinner and costs less. The other has light black surface with cracks, is thicker, and costs more. You can use either one. In this book black mushrooms are measured before they are soaked.

BLACK MUSHROOMS

These are imported from Taiwan or Japan in cans, peeled, chunked, and boiled and ready to use. Japanese canned whole bamboo shoots are more tender than Taiwan's and the price is higher. They have a white powder in the center between the layers which should be rinsed off. Dried bamboo shoots and pickled bamboo shoots are not very popular here and are not used in the recipes of this book. In China there are many kinds of

BAMBOO SHOOTS

7

bamboo shoots according to seasons and sizes. Bamboo grows in a warm climate and the shoots are edible only when they are tender, before they grow up to become bamboo. Not every kind of bamboo shoot is good for eating.

Winter Bamboo Shoots The husks are hard and wrapped very tight. After they are dug out of the ground they can be kept for weeks in a cold place.

Early Spring Bamboo Shoots These are tender and small, about the size of a thumb. The growing season is very short.

Spring Bamboo Shoots There are two varieties of spring bamboo shoots in China which are good for eating. They grow fast, especially after spring rains. To describe anything that grows fast, the Chinese say *It is like spring bamboo shoots after rain.* 雨後春筍

One of the two varieties is about one or two inches in diameter with light and smooth husks; the other kind is three to eight inches in diameter, as large as a small baby, with dark and hairy husks. The hairy husks give them better protection. They are often shipped out of town for sale. My mother told me when hairy bamboo shoots are shipped down the river they still grow even though they have been cut away from their roots. So the shippers have to throw some away in the river while sailing to keep the boat from bursting. Summer bamboo shoots are bitter and not popular. In summer time, people dig out new roots to eat like shoots.

WATER CHESTNUTS These are grown in water fields like rice. The part for eating is the bulb, a dark purplish brown and of the size of a walnut. In stores they sometimes appear quite muddy, but that is the way to prevent them from drying out. The meat is white or creamy

8

white. If you find the meat becomes yellow or brown and has a strong odor, that indicates it is rotten and should not be used. If it is only partially spoiled, you can cut off the rotted part and use the remaining white meat. To prepare, wash off mud, peel off the skin, and use meat whole, sliced, or diced. Fresh, they are sweeter and more crunchy than canned water chestnuts which are peeled and cooked, and usually packed whole. For restaurant use, they are also packed sliced and diced in large cans.

Remember, to keep the texture crunchy, bamboo shoots and water chestnuts should never be frozen. Left-over shoots and chestnuts should be kept in water in the refrigerator and the water changed every two or three days. In this way they can be kept for weeks without getting sour.

BEAN SPROUTS

They are sprouts of Mung Bean, a kind of tiny green beans. Many Chinese cookbooks mention them as pea sprouts. Since they are sprouts of mung beans and are known in the market as bean sprouts, it is better to call them that to avoid confusion.

Fresh bean sprouts are available daily in Chinese groceries and the price is very reasonable and steady. If you compare fresh bean sprouts with canned, you will know why I do not recommend the canned bean sprouts. If you cannot get them from a store and have no time to grow your own, then shred the white thick part of lettuce as a substitute in Cantonese fried rice, or any dish requiring only a small amount. (For how to grow bean sprouts at home see page 52.) There are also soy bean sprouts known as "yellow bean sprouts", which are very popular in China but not here. Occasionally they can be purchased in Chinese groceries.

BEAN THREAD

This is better known as Chinese vermicelli, or cellophane noodles, which is made from mung bean into very thin and smooth, translucent noodles. Bean thread should be softened before use by soaking in warm water for 5 to 15 minutes. Because it is so thin and is cooked in the making, it should not be cooked long; heating slightly or dipping in boiling soup is enough. Otherwise it will become gluey and lose its smooth texture.

CHINESE HAM

Most banquet dishes require a small amount of Chinese ham for improving flavor and aroma and for decoration and garnishing. It is almost impossible to get Chinese ham here; the best substitute is Smithfield Ham, of which the older and more red in color is better.

There are four ways to cut the cooked ham: slice, shred, dice, or mince, all depending on the dish you are preparing. It is the Chinese way to cook ham first before using in quick–stirring cooked dishes. Because only a small amount of ham is needed for a dish, it is better to cut off a big slice of ham each time (1″-2″ in thickness). In Chinese groceries, Smithfield ham may be purchased in desired slices. Peel off outside dark coating with sharp knife, scrub skin (or cut off the skin), steam cleaned ham for 20 minutes per inch thickness of slice, or put thin (about 1″) sliced ham in an aluminum dish or sheet on top of rice which is in the process of simmering. The juice of the ham is very tasty and can be used with ham. Left-over cooked ham should be wrapped to prevent dryness and can be kept in refrigerator for 1-2 weeks. The ham bone and gristle cooked with soup add more flavor.

DRIED SHRIMP

There is a kind of small, dried, shelled salt water shrimp from New Orleans, U.S.A., on the gulf coast, but only the Chinese know how to enjoy them. It is good to be eaten just as it

10

is. My son, Henry, likes to nibble on them while watching television. These dried shrimps are really one of the wonders in Chinese cooking. They can be cooked with vegetables as a meat, or added to salad, celery and Chinese celery cabbage to enrich the flavor. They are also used to replace meat or ham in soups. They are easy to store in a jar in a dry cool place, and do not need refrigeration for a long, long time. If they get too dry, then soak them in a little amount of water or sherry. They even can be sprinkled with sherry and steamed to make them soft, and chopped for garnish on salads (about 1 to 2 TBS dried shrimps with 1 tsp sherry).

Because of the convenience in storing and cooking, dried shrimps are widely used in all Chinese families in China and here. Also they are comparatively inexpensive as only a small amount of them is used.

蝦
米

WINTER MELON

This is a very large-sized melon for cooking only. It has green skin with a white powdered surface, which is perhaps the reason for its name, and it has little light brown seeds. It is sold in Chinese groceries in slices by the pound. For preparing, peel off skin with sharp knife and scrape out seeds, then slice or chunk the melon and cook with other ingredients.

A very popular dish cooked with winter melon is Winter Melon and Ham Soup. (see page 91.) A more exciting dish is Winter Melon Bowl. The latter requires a small whole winter melon which is hard to obtain here. This recipe will be in my next book. Winter melon should be tenderly cooked in any kind of dish. Fermented winter melon is a famous dish in Ning-po 寧 波 near Shanghai. It is like blue cheese, tasty and smelly. Please do not try to make it without a proper recipe.

冬
瓜

WOOD EARS

This is a kind of fungus growing on trees. It is black and gelatinous. Now it comes dried from Japan. For preparing, soften by soaking in boiling water in large bowl for 10-15 minutes. Softened wood ears expand 5-6 times in size. Because it is gelatinous, do not cook it too long. The wood ears are often cooked together with golden needles in soup or most vegetable dishes. Cantonese call wood ears "cloud ears."

GOLDEN NEEDLES

A kind of yellow flower like Tiger Lily, it comes from Hong Kong in a dried pressed block by the pound. To prepare, soften golden needles in the same way as black mushrooms. Sometimes the flowers (rather, buds) have hard stems which should be removed before cooking. Generally we line up the softened golden needles together, then cut them because they are quite long.

BEAN CURD

Bean curd is an important ingredient of food in China. It is very nutritious and low in price. It is also a very important ingredient in vegetarian dishes. Buddhists require a strict vegetable diet; bean curd gives them the necessary protein. Bean curd looks like cheese cake and is white in color. It is made by grinding softened soy beans with lots of water into a kind of soy bean milk which is actually served as milk in China. Then the milk is coagulated into a soft cake. Because the grinding and setting require plenty of time and experience, bean curd is never made at home, but only in special stores both in China and in the United States. Bean curd may also be served uncooked with soy sauce and sesame oil as a side dish.

Frozen bean curd becomes spongy and has a very different texture. It is excellent to be used in what we call *FIRE POT*. It is a pot with a chimney in its center. Charcoal is put in the lower part of the chimney to keep the soup in the pot boiling, to cook the raw ingredients in the soup, or to keep the food warm.

12

Chinese Seasonings and Spices

CHINESE SEASONING AND SPICES INTRODUCED AND recommended in this chapter are limited to those used in recipes in this book.

COOKING OIL

In China people prefer to use lard in cooking as the Europeans prefer butter. Lard gives rich flavor and clear color. That is the reason lard is very expensive in China. I was so surprised to know lard was so inexpensive here, when I came to this country. Nowadays more and more doctors are proving that animal fat is not healthy to eat. So I gave up lard in home cooking as well as at the restaurant. When I see so many doctors eating at our restaurant, especially when Dr. Paul Dudley White comes, I am encouraged to improve my dishes and my recipes, not just in flavor but also in nutrition.

Many people ask me about what is the right kind of oil to cook with. It is true that the right kind of oil is very important in a good dish. There are three kinds of vegetable oils for cooking in China:

Peanut oil: It is the next best to lard, tastes richer than other kinds of vegetable oil. Very good for deep frying. It turns cloudy in very cold temperature but does not change in flavor.

Soy bean oil: It is not so popular as peanut oil. Recently in

13

this country many doctors have recommended it for use in cooking. I think the soy bean oil is lighter, but it is not for sale in supermarkets yet.

Chinese cabbage seed oil: This oil is only available in southern China. We use a lot of this kind in my home town.

Of course sesame seed oil is very popular but it is used mostly in seasoning and garnishing, not in cooking. (See page 21)

There are many kinds of cooking oil in this country. Peanut oil, cotton seed oil, and corn oil are good. Soy bean oil is also good but not easy to buy yet. Some kinds of vegetable oil, which have a special odor, should not be used, as the odor will spoil the true flavor of the food. Butter, margarine, olive oil, and cream type of vegetable shortening are not suitable. The best kind of oil to use in Chinese cooking should be odorless, tasteless, and clear. Chinese cabbage and Chinese celery cabbage hearts cooked in chicken fat is a very famous dish in China. (See page 169). Chicken fat improves flavor in certain kinds of vegetable dishes and also gives a pretty yellow color on top of the dish. I understand Jewish people also like to use chicken fat.

SOY SAUCE

醬
油

Soy sauce is made of soy beans, wheat flour, salt, water and plenty of sunshine. At first the steamed dough, which is made of soy beans and flour, is allowed to ferment, then the fermented dough is soaked in large open earthenware urns with salt and water. The urn is left in an open space under sunshine for a few weeks and is covered in case of rain. The sunshine makes the mixture turn brown. The liquid is soy sauce.

Please do not try to make it yourself. This requires an expert's technical know-how.

There are two kinds of soy sauce available in the United States:

14

Most of the ingredients are salt, water and coloring. Its color is grayish dark brown and it does not have the soy bean aroma. It is usually saltier than the imported Chinese soy sauce.

The Japanese make very good soy sauce. The color is light and the taste is salty. It is good for table dipping. We never pour soy sauce over a whole plate of food as I have seen many Americans do.

There are also two kinds of soy sauce imported from Hong Kong. That which is light colored and a little salty to the taste is for table use. The dark colored is for cooking such as Shanghai ham, soy sauce fish, etc. The dark soy sauce gives a bright dark brown color. The best Shanghai ham and other soy sauce dishes should be shiny and dark brown.

There are no standards in color and saltiness. It is hard for me to tell you which is the best one to buy. Even in the same bottle, soy sauce at the bottom is saltier than on the top. Sometimes poor soy sauce can spoil the whole dish. I bottle my own special mixture for my cooking school. All my recipes are based on this kind of soy sauce. For your convenience, you may order some from me.

Most Americans think that there is soy sauce in every Chinese dish. Actually, we do use a considerable amount of soy sauce in cooking, but to preserve nice color and light delicate taste of food, we very often omit soy sauce or use a very small amount in such dishes as white chicken meat, fish, shrimp, and delicate green vegetables. The right amount of soy sauce depends upon what is to be cooked and how it is to be served.

Almost all Chinese families serve rice as Americans serve bread. This is not true, however, in North China where people serve things made of wheat flour such as noodles, steamed rolls, etc., more frequently than rice. Dishes to be served with rice are a little saltier and usually cooked with soy sauce. Dishes made of delicate ingredients and served at banquet parties are lighter and usually cooked with little or no soy sauce.

WINE

Wine in Chinese cookery is very important. Chinese always add a small amount of wine to meat and especially to sea food to neutralize strong odors, not primarily for its flavor as in French cookery. We do have many dishes using a large amount of wine to marinate food, such as wined chicken, etc.

The most popular Chinese wine is made of rice. Those provinces where rice grows also have a climate suitable for brewing wine. Wine is stored in large size and small-mouthed urns sealed with mud. Many farmers brew their own wine. In Hsao-hsing 紹興 villagers brew a large amount of wine when a baby girl is born. They bury the urns underground until the girl's wedding day when the wine is taken out and served at the old-fashioned wedding feast which lasts several days.

酒

The best wine is clear and light in color. The high grade is for drinking and is preferably served warm. The low grade is for cooking. It is impossible to get Chinese wine here. The most advisable substitute is *pale dry sherry*. Do not use cream sherry which has too strong a flavor.

Another well-known Chinese wine Kaoliang 高粱 is made from a kind of grain (like sorghum) called Kaoliang. The best Kaoliang is manufactured in Manchuria, clear like water and strong like Vodka. We add Kaoliang in many vegetable dishes. The famous Szechuan pickles need Kaoliang to improve their crunchy texture, taste and aroma.

GINGER ROOT

The ginger plant is grown in a warm climate. The part used for cooking is the root, which has a grayish light brown skin and inside is a yellowish beige color. It has a strong sharp aroma. Most

16

ginger root sold in the United States is mostly from Hawaii. Fresh ginger root is obtainable year round in any Chinese grocery. Ginger root should be kept fresh for a few weeks in a refrigerator. *Never freeze it*. Cleaned and sliced ginger root, peeled or not, can be kept for months if soaked in dry sherry. Mrs. Y. W. Lee cooks chopped ginger root in peanut oil and keeps it in a jar in the refrigerator for a few months. The best way to clean ginger root is with a brush; slice or chop it before preserving it for easy use.

In Chinese cookery, whenever meat or seafood is cooked, ginger root is put in. The strong aroma of ginger root not only neutralizes the odors but is also believed to absorb any evil in the food. Therefore Chinese do not eat ginger slices in dishes. Customarily, ginger root slices are used to neutralize odors and minced ginger root for flavoring food. Very often minced ginger root and scallion or crushed garlic mixed in soy sauce are used as dipping sauce on the table. Boil crushed or minced fresh ginger root and sweeten the liquor with brown sugar to make so-called Ginger Tea (1 walnut-sized piece crushed, or 1 heaping tablespoon minced ginger root, makes 4 cups of ginger tea) which is good for a cold and excellent to serve after football games! We always serve minced ginger root with vinegar, soy sauce, etc., for dipping steamed crabs. After steamed crabs a cup of ginger tea is always served. Old Chinese wives say that rubbing ginger root on bare spots of the scalp makes new hair grow. You might be interested in trying this on your husband's bald head. Please let me know the results.

Washed preserved ginger root may be used instead of fresh ginger. Do not use ginger powder. Use ginger root juice for delicate dishes such as shrimp ball, etc. Prepare juice by squeezing minced ginger root through a garlic squeezer, cheese cloth, or with your finger tips.

Ginger shoots are tender and less sharp. They are delicious

17

when cooked with meat or pickled in soy sauce, but the season is very short, and they are hard to get.

SCALLION

In China scallions are very often used with ginger root. Chinese use scallions in two ways, as the French use onion and parsley: to cook with food and to garnish food. Northern Chinese like to eat them raw dipped in bean paste. Hoi Sin sauce also makes a good dip for raw scallions. The scallions which grow in the north are larger and more tender than those from any other places.

Certain dishes require a large amount of scallions prepared with soy sauce. Many people are very fond of scallions cooked in this way. We usually remove the scallion and ginger root, when they are used for flavoring, before serving, for a better, neater appearance, particularly in party dishes. For easy removing, we sometimes twist a whole scallion into a knot. In here I suggest that you fold the whole scallion 2″ or 3″ long, tying it together with thread like a bouquet, as the scallion from the refrigerator is too crisp to be knotted. For garnishing, scallions are often minced or chopped. Some people prefer to use fine shredded scallions. We use the nice green part of scallions for garnishing and the white tender part to eat raw.

Heated oil poured over minced scallions improves the aroma and will make a nice salad dressing or table dip.

Rotted scallion has a terrible odor; scallion wrapped in a dry paper towel will keep fresh longer in the refrigerator.

GARLIC

Northern Chinese serve minced garlic as Americans serve horse radish. They like to use crushed garlic in most of their dishes. People near Shanghai usually cannot stand garlic's strong flavor.

18

Garlic is good to use for covering the strong odor of food such as lamb, fish, etc. Do not use it with delicate ingredients. Pickled garlic is very popular in China. Crushed garlic with soy sauce and sesame oil makes a wonderful dipping sauce for plain cooked meat. (See page 57)

We grow peeled garlic cloves in water or earth indoors during the winter months. The minced leaves are then used as a garnish for soups and other dishes.

HOT PEPPER

We often use hot pepper flakes for cooking, hot pepper paste and hot pepper oil for table dipping. (See page 56.) In some of the provinces in China they add hot pepper to almost any dish and even mix it with rice or noodles. As a rule, people who live in places with warm climates like hot pepper. The hot pepper stimulates appetite and helps perspiration. They eat hot pepper as you drink coffee; they feel uncomfortable if without it. Hot pepper may be added to any dish while cooking, but it is especially suitable for quick-stirring dishes. It is safer to put hot pepper flakes in the pan after the first ingredient is added. Be careful not to let hot pepper flakes burn. The dark spots will spoil the appearance of the dish, particularly in light-colored food.

辣
椒

Shredded and diced fresh hot pepper may be substituted for green pepper or hot pepper flakes. It is better to wear rubber gloves while taking out the seeds from the pepper. Otherwise your finger tips will burn for a whole day. (If you prefer your dish to be extra hot then keep the seeds.)

Szechuan people make delicious hot pepper paste with hot peppers, beans, spices and seasoning. We use the hot pepper paste as relish, table dipping or even in cooking.

The hot pepper oil is very easy to make at home at any time. When it is freshly prepared, it has a wonderful aroma. If you like hot food, probably you can not live without it.

19

STAR ANISE

Once I showed star anise to Mr. Leslie Browning of S. S. Pierce's (also known as Mr. Epicure), who said he had never seen it in the United States. Star anise is a seed formation of eight cloves which look like a star. They are so fragile that in recipes I count them by cloves. We generally use star anise in dishes like Shanghai ham and Shanghai duck that are cooked with a lot of soy sauce. If the recipe calls for quite a few anise cloves it is better to tie them loosely in cheese cloth for easy removal after cooking. Star Anise is available in most Chinese groceries.

If star anise is not obtainable then use anise seed for an emergency substitute. (Take 1 tsp of anise seed and tie in two or three layers of cheese cloth loosely).

If you like garlic, then use it for substitute, about 1 to 2 cloves, crushed for more flavor.

CHINESE PEPPER CORN

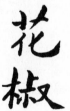

It looks like black pepper corn but is quite hollow inside with only one small seed. Most of the time the shell and seed have already been separated. Chinese pepper corn has a strong appetizing aroma and is commonly toasted and ground to mix with salt for deep fried food as a kind of dry dipping. Toast with salt and rub on meat to make preserved meat — ham and salty chicken, etc. Chinese pepper corn is added to Chinese pickles to enrich the aroma. Chinese pepper corn is very hard to get here. The best substitute is black pepper corn.

BLACK BEANS

These beans have been fermented and mixed with salt and spice and stored for a long period. They are very tasty and salty and black in color. Adding one tablespoon or more of minced or crushed black beans in food brings out more flavor. Minced meat, garlic and lots of black beans make a kind of relish for the table. Store black beans in a jar or plastic bag to preserve moisture and prevent odors.

20

There are two kinds of beans that make paste: fava beans and soy beans. Fava bean is sweeter and soy bean paste is more salty. In this country they are both imported from Hong Kong and Japan. The bean paste which comes from Hong Kong is in two forms: Bean Sauce — bean paste with halves of soy bean (yellow bean) Ground Bean Sauce — bean paste in smoother form. In this book, only the ground bean paste is used. Sometimes it is not available in 1 lb cans, then you have to mash the beans into a smooth paste. (5 lb can is too much for you to use at home.) I prefer to use Japanese-made bean paste called Miso, which is shipped from Japan in wooden drums and does not have a metal smell. There are two varieties of Miso, white and dark. I mix them half and half. You can keep bean paste in a jar in the refrigerator for months.

It is imported in cans from Hong Kong, a kind of thick sauce made of bean, sugar, salt and spices, to be used at the table or in cooking. It has been widely used by Cantonese and in Chinese restaurants here. People who like heavy and spicy food enjoy it. After opening a can, the Hoi Sin sauce can be stored for a long time in a jar with a tight cover, like jams or jellies.

This oil, made of toasted white sesame seeds, has an appetizing aroma and is golden brown in color. Because the sesame seeds have been toasted, the oil burns more easily, so it is very seldom used for cooking. Use it like salad oil or for garnishing dishes.

Western cooks would be surprised to see how sugar is used in Chinese cooking. It is an important seasoning, especially in the Shanghai style of cooking. Almost as a rule, if a large amount

BEAN PASTE

醬

HOI SIN SAUCE

海鮮醬

SESAME SEED OIL

麻油

SUGAR

糖

21

of soy sauce is used, some sugar is added to improve the flavor, just the way you add salt to your cakes and cookies. The amount of sugar to use varies according to styles of cooking and taste. My home town is near Shanghai; we use more sugar than others. Therefore the amount of sugar the recipes call for is the most you should use. I say to your taste, that means you could decrease but not increase.

In China we use crystal sugar (rock candy) in Shanghai duck and ham, etc. to make the dish shining and clear. Here I like to use light brown sugar for more flavor.

OYSTER SAUCE

A kind of dark brown sauce which is made of oyster and seasoning. There are two kinds of oyster sauce in the United States: domestic and imported. Of course the imported oyster sauce is better and more expensive. People who like oyster sauce use it in much the same way as soy sauce. It is particularly good with quick-stirring and dark-colored dishes, such as beef dishes, etc. Oyster sauce is very tasty and salty. Reduce the salt or soy sauce if oyster sauce is added. Oyster sauce also makes a wonderful dipping sauce for the table.

MONOSODIUM GLUTAMATE POWDER

My father's good friend Mr. Wu was the founder of the first and largest factory in China which makes the famous Ve-Tsin. I had several relatives on his staff. Ve-Tsin is a white powder or crystal, a by-product of soy bean and wheat refining. Monosodium glutamate (MSG) powder is widely used in canned food everywhere now, but we used it many years before. Many brands are on the market (notably Accent and MSG). We use it by adding a small amount (¼ to ½ tsp) to dishes for improving flavor, and it works wonderfully in making bland foods taste better. Although MSG is specified in many of my recipes, its use is optional and can be omitted without further changes.

22

This is a group of spices which are ground together into a powder. These are anise seed, cinnamon, licorice, clove, ginger, nutmeg, etc. The mixture is used in dishes requiring strong spice flavor. In this book, it is used in barbecued spare ribs and pork strips. If you are unable to get the spice powder already prepared in a Chinese grocery, then use mixed cinnamon, clove, ginger and nutmeg powder for a substitute. (Only a very small amount of these is used, about ¼ tsp altogether.)

CHINESE FIVE SPICES POWDER

五香粉

This is a kind of molasses with a very dark color and is the ingredient used in making Fried Rice Cantonese Style brown. It is available in most super markets. Otherwise, use Kitchen Bouquet or Gravy Master for a substitute. I use a small amount of it to make right color of the Peking Duck.

BROWN GRAVY SYRUP

珠油

Utensils for Chinese Cooking

I STRONGLY FEEL THAT IT IS NOT NECESSARY TO get special utensils just for cooking Chinese dishes. It is fun and easier to use Chinese made tools on sale at Chinese groceries, but they are not absolutely necessary. I have often brought only a shopping bag of ingredients to cook at my American friends' homes for a banquet party of ten or more. We tested my recipes to see how they would work out in an American kitchen. My philosophy: We should control the surroundings, not let the surroundings control us. Of course, fine utensils make cooking easier.

Chinese Cleaver

According to my experience, three items are very important in a kitchen: a large sharp knife, a good hardwood cutting board, and a heavy smooth skillet. The Chinese do not have knives on the table, so most foods are cut in bite size, or large pieces of meat are cooked tender enough to pick up by chopsticks.

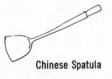

Chinese Spatula

We do need a good sharp chef's knife and good cutting board to cut easily and neatly in preparation. Stainless steel knives are usually too flexible and difficult to sharpen. Any rough bottom surface of earthenware can be used as an emergency knife sharpener. Chinese cleavers may scare you but are very handy.

Chinese Scoop

Since the Chinese dishes are usually cooked by quick stirring, it is better to use a large, heavy skillet or frying pan which holds the heat. If the skillet is also smooth and seasoned by use, less food will stick.

24

A large steamer is required for many Chinese dishes. Set a rack at the bottom of a large pot, the wider the better; raise the rack by putting a metal ring under it, the size of a coffee can with both ends removed. You could make one from a used large can. Sometimes you can get a round rack with about 3″-high legs. Add water to the pot, put it on the heat and cover it. This makes a steamer. The level of water should be at least 2″-3″ lower than the food, so the water will not be boiling into food. Between the food and the cover there should be enough room for the steam to circulate freely. If the cooking period is quite long, then add more water to the pot to prevent the water from drying out and the food from burning. I find a safe way to take the steamed food out from steamer is as follows:

1. Turn off flame.
2. Take off cover from steamer, wait a second to let the hot steam go, and
3. Put on the kitchen rubber gloves and take the food out.

Chinese Frying Pan — WOCK

The Chinese frying pan, called "Wock" by the Cantonese, is easier for stirring, but not suitable for an electric stove.

The following items will make your Chinese cooking easier:

Large enameled iron pots are good to simmer food, and keep warm in the oven, and serve on the table. They should be 3-4 qt. capacity.

Wock Cover

Shallow pressure cooker is good to use for quick stirring, especially for foods which require a deeper skillet. Excellent for vegetables with loose leaves.

Two colanders, one large and one small, and one strainer.

Wooden spoons for stirring rice and soft food.

Good, solid stirring and straining spoons and spatula.

Extra mixing bowls or large measuring cups.

Chopsticks are handy for loosening and mixing food.

A tweezer is useful for pulling feathers from birds or hair from pork skins.

Ring to fit Wock for western stoves

An old-fashioned can opener is necessary for opening the square Chinese food cans.

A garlic squeezer is good for ginger juice.

Empty glass jars with wide openings and unrusted covers are very useful to store canned Chinese food and ingredients.

Plastic bags are good for storing food, preventing dryness, and take less room in the refrigerator.

Racks which are used to cool cookies or cakes are useful to roast spare ribs and warm deep fried foods in the oven.

An exhaust kitchen fan is a great help in keeping the kitchen clean and fresh, especially when quick stirring cooking and also when cooking American food.

Preparations for Chinese Cooking

IN MY COOKING CLASSES, I ALWAYS WANT MY students to know why and how. In this way they can better understand the steps in cooking and will be able to work out the best in different circumstances and to figure out the best items to use as substitute ingredients.

When you use my recipes in this book, you should read the opening chapters first; then read each recipe two or three times before you start to cook it. Sometimes the dish does not come out right because someone was too hasty to read the recipe thoroughly. Cooking is an art which is used daily; if you use my recipes, it is my duty to provide you the right information and steps in a new way of cooking. If you follow my instruction carefully, the dishes should come out all right. You are the one to make the dishes successful. If anything goes wrong or right there must be a reason. In some things the reason for failure is beyond our control, but in cooking success is always under our control.

Since labour is plentiful in China, most dishes are prepared by long hours of work to make the food easy to eat and nice to look at. The situation is not the same here, so the recipes in this book do not require too much work. Generally Chinese cooking needs more preparing and less cooking than any other kind of cookery. Therefore proper preparation is very important. Most of the preparation could be done hours, even days, ahead. It is better to store cut up ingredients in the refrigerator with a tight plastic wrap covering to prevent drying out.

If you wash vegetables ahead, you should drain them very well before storing them in refrigerator. They stay better in a plastic bag with holes, as the vegetables will rot if they are too wet. It is better *not* to wash the vegetables with loose leaves too long ahead, as they will wilt and rot easily.

It is advisable to sear or scald big pieces of meat or birds, which are cooked whole, as soon as possible. They will keep better and longer in the refrigerator.

For such dishes as Shanghai ham and duck, which require long periods of simmering, the cooking can be divided over several days.

CUTTING

Since there are no knives on the table, most Chinese foods are cut into bite size. Ingredients should be cut uniformly to assure even cooking and nice and neat looking dishes. Meat should be cut across the grain to improve tenderness. Fat and gristle should be removed before cutting. For easy cutting, freeze meat slightly.

In cutting big and round items, such as whole bamboo shoots and onion, into small pieces, the easy way is to cut the item lengthwise in half and lay the flat side down, then slice, shred, etc. Every cut should be neat and thorough.

In China we use the cleaver to cut ingredients, but I have found that the Chinese cutting method works just as well with a western chef's knife. The cutting method:

The left hand holds and presses the item to be cut in place on the cutting board. The right hand holds the knife to cut the item uniformly into small pieces as needed. The right hand with the knife goes forward, and the left hand goes backward in a uniform motion. If the item is small use the thumb of left hand

28

to push the end of the item instead of the whole left hand going backward. Probably in beginning you will cut slowly but with practice you will speed up and enjoy it. The first joint of left hand will protect the finger tips which should be bent back a little and the finger nails will help hold the item tightly. The knife should be lifted not too high, just above the item, with the side of the blade just touching the first joint.

Dice — about ½″ on a side. First cut the article in ½″ wide strips. Then lay the strips together and cut the row of strips across into squares.

Cube — is about 1″ on a side.

Chunk — is 1½″ to 2″ on a side.

Slice — is 1½ to 2 inches long, 1″ wide, and ⅛″ to ¼″ thick. Slice diagonally to adjust sizes.

Shred

To cut in thin strips. First cut the article into thin slices, keep them in place, then pat them flat and cut the slices diagonally into uniform thin strips.

Chop

In China the meat grinder is not as common as here. We chop meat finely instead of grinding. Of course we should use the grinder for meat, but for small amount of vegetables it is better to chop by hand. Hand-chopped vegetables will be juicy and neat. Chop in this book means to cut articles into fine pieces the size of a pea.

Mince

Very fine pieces, about ¼ of a pea.

Rolling Cut

Is a special way of Chinese cutting to cut something round and long into large pieces, such as carrot, cucumber, etc. Turn the article to be cut with left hand while your right hand holds the knife and cut the article diagonally. Change the angle of the knife to adjust for even-sized pieces.

29

Splitting

To make thinner slices and shreds from small or flat pieces of an article, lay the article flat on the cutting board and hold it with pressure from the fingers of your left hand. Now cut through, holding the blade of the knife parallel to the board and splitting carefully between the board and your fingers. If it is a thicker piece then make two or three even splits.

WASHING

In Chinese cookery, since we cook vegetables with little water or without water, proper washing is important. Wash off the starch of uncooked rice by changing water two or three times. This makes rice more fluffy. Wash the sand off vegetables with large loose leaves such as spinach, Chinese cabbage, etc. by washing them in large amount of water three or four times. The best way is to wash the outside leaves individually and rub off the sand with fingers or brush, especially at the ends of stalks. (I also wash packaged spinach again and very often find sand and weeds inside.) To wash root vegetables, such as ginger, use a brush. Rinse green peppers before cutting them, so the water will not remain in the pockets.

Sand in the food will spoil the whole dish, so the careful washing of vegetables is most essential in preparation. Sometimes you will feel, when stirring the food from bottom of the pan while it is cooking, that there is still sand. Then be sure not to serve the bottom part of the gravy, as the sand always settles on the bottom of the liquid.

PARBOILING

Sometimes we parboil vegetables to prepare banquet dishes, such as broccoli, green bean, green pea and so on, to shorten cooking time. Cut and wash the ingredients first. Boil water in a large pot. The amount of water should allow the ingredients to swim around freely. Stir the ingredients into the water, which will stop boiling when ingredients are added. Continue stirring for even cooking. If the vegetable is to be eaten crisp such as broccoli, celery, etc., take out from the water before it boils again. For vegetables such as green beans, peas, and carrots, that cannot be eaten raw or take a longer time to cook, take out after the water starts boiling again. Pour the parboiled ingredients with water into colander, rinse or soak the ingredients in cold water until thoroughly cooled. Then store in refrigerator covered and ready to use. We often parboil vegetables to serve as salad. (See page 165 to 178.)

SEARING OR SCALDING

As western cooks often sear poultry or meat by browning them in oil or fat, or in hot oven, Chinese cooks accomplish the searing by immersing the birds or large piece of meat in boiling water. As soon as the water boils again, take out the bird or meat and rinse it in cold water. Then pull out the hair or feathers. In this way the bird or meat is seared, and the skin is shrunk so the hair and feathers will stand up and be easy to pull out. Also rinse off the outside blood and fat and clean bird's cavity. The bird and meat will be much cleaner and neat. The gravy or the soup will be clearer too. Fine hair of bird should be singed over flame or high heat. (Small pieces of meat should not be seared or scalded. All fat and gristle should be trimmed, although ground meat needs a certain amount of fat to make it taste tender and juicy.)

Chinese Cooking Methods

炒燜
煮蒸

QUICK STIRRING

FOLLOWING ARE THE MAJOR WAYS OF COOKING Chinese food in this book:

Using a small amount of oil in heated skillet or frying pan, cook cut-up pieces of ingredients over high heat by constantly stirring for a short period (one to a few minutes). This is like French saute. The skillet or pan should be large enough so the ingredients are not crowded; this not only makes stirring easier but also cooks more evenly. Most quick-stirring cooked dishes should be served immediately. This way cooked vegetables will be crisp and crunchy.

Chinese dishes are usually cooked meat and vegetables together so the vegetables will be enriched with the meat flavor. Many of my American students find out this is a wonderful way to make children eat some vegetables; also it is very economical. If the dish is cooked in quick-stirring method, we always cook the meat and vegetables separately, then mix them together in the pan. I like to suggest quick-stirring the vegetable first, taking it out and using the same pan to cook the meat mixture. If the pan has some burned spots after cooking vegetables, wipe them off with a paper towel. Sometimes if you cook the meat mixture first, the pan needs to be washed before cooking the vegetable. With the busy American life, I think we should be lazy if we can.

All ingredients in the same dish should be of even size and

32

shape. Vegetables may be parboiled before quick stirring. Small pieces of meat should be mixed with wine and cornstarch or soy sauce before cooking. Pork should be cooked longer, until no more blood comes out.

It is necessary to have all ingredients prepared and placed in reaching distance beside the stove, because the constant stirring makes you stay next to the stove. In case the ingredients get too dry, pour a little water in to prevent burning. If you lose control, lift the skillet off the heat immediately. As soon as the ingredients are cooked, lift off heat then remove from skillet or pan for immediate serving.

The first ingredients put into oil should be as *dry* as possible to prevent oil from spitting. Add salt first into oil if ingredients require salt.

BOILING

To boil in heavy liquid, you should reduce heat when the liquid starts boiling, or keep the cover open a little; otherwise the liquid will boil over. If the liquid boils over, the best way is to take off the cover first or to remove the pan from heat, or add a small amount of cold water. As soon as the liquid boils you should reduce the heat for slow boiling or simmering. Active boiling will make the liquid creamy and evaporate quickly, and will take longer to cook food to the right tenderness. (Gentle strength always goes a long way!)

SIMMER

In Chinese cooking, to simmer means to cook food over low heat in liquid, boiling very slowly, with just one or two bubblings at a time. Large ingredients like Shanghai ham need to simmer a long time to be tender. Good clear soup or broth should be reduced to a simmer as soon as it comes to a boil.

33

BASTE   After ingredients are cooked tender, if there is still a lot of liquid, you may use cornstarch to thicken it. The usual family way, especially for a big piece of meat, is to take the cover off, turn the heat higher and let the liquid boil and evaporate. While doing this one should turn the ingredients occasionally and spoon the liquid on to the ingredients for even color and saltiness and to prevent the food from burning.

STEAM   Steaming food is a very common way in Chinese cooking. The food being steamed should be out of reach of the boiling water. The pot or steamer should be large enough so the steam will circulate freely around the food. It is necessary to have a fitted cover which can be tightly closed while steaming. In many ways steaming food in China is like roasting food here, because there is no oven in the Chinese family kitchen. For steaming, the water in the pot or steamer should be boiling actively. (About the steamer, see page 25)

PRESSURE COOKING   It is very handy to speed the dishes which require a long period of simmering by using a pressure cooker. The pressure cooker does a better job in cooking chunks of meat than the large piece of meat such as whole fresh ham, shoulder and butt. These are often over-cooked outside and even bloody inside, especially when the piece is ice cold. It is advisable to take a large piece of meat out of the refrigerator about 1-2 hours before cooking.

I like to cook meat and poultry that needs a long time simmering in the pressure cooker without putting the pressure cap on, since the cover is so tight. This cooks the food tender more quickly than any other kind of pot, and needs less water. The food will not burn easily as the cooker is quite heavy. And I can also open the cover at anytime to check the food.

34

Cooking food in large amounts of oil is a way to make food taste better; it seals in the flavor and crisps the outside. In deep frying, always make sure the item to be cooked is floating and swimming freely in the oil. The most easy way to test whether the oil is hot or not is to put in a small piece of bread crust, ginger or egg roll skin (when making egg roll or wonton) into the oil. If the oil foams actively along the item it means the oil is hot enough to fry. Always drain deep fry foods before serving, or cook again with other ingredients.

If deep frying a small amount of food, then use smaller pan and use less oil.

Cornstarch in Chinese Cooking

THE RIGHT USE OF CORNSTARCH IS ESSENTIAL IN Chinese cooking. As in China we do not use cookbooks, there are no measuring spoons and cups in the kitchen. All the cooking is done by trial and error both at home and in the restaurant. In a skill where so much is done by custom and where many of the traditions are so unfamiliar, I feel it is especially important for me to make things clear for you, tell you why and how, establish rules for your guidance.

The starch made from the fruit of a kind of water-plant in China is the best to use. It is more clear after cooking. In this country cornstarch is the best substitute. (Arrowroot is good, too.)

Cornstarch is used in three ways:

COATING   Any small pieces of meat, including poultry and seafood, should be mixed with cornstarch before cooking. We add the *dry* cornstarch to the meat because the sherry — or soy sauce — and the moisture of meat will mix very well. The cornstarch gives the meat a light coating which not only makes the meat taste tender but also holds more flavor from the gravy. We should give the meat mixture a last-second stirring before it goes into the pan, as the wet cornstarch is always set in the bottom.

THICKENING   You use flour to thicken your gravy; we always use corn-

36

starch to do the job, because the flour makes the gravy cloudy and also too heavy and floury in taste. The thickness of the gravy and soup depends on the amount of cornstarch used, which varies in different dishes. Sweet and sour dishes should be thicker. Soup should be lighter. Of course, more or less cornstarch should be used according to the amount of liquid to be thickened. Many American families prefer the dishes with a lot of gravy. They may add more water — or stock — and cornstarch; salt, or soy sauce to taste. If you add cornstarch it *must* be mixed well with cold water and stirred quickly into the food while cooking, and served immediately.

The cornstarch will turn watery in leftovers; a little more cornstarch mixed with water may be added when re-heating.

HOLDING

The cornstarch also works wonderfully for holding the ground meat together and keeping the moisture in, in dishes such as lion head, etc. I add cornstarch with some milk to hamburger and meat loaf, to make them taste better.

Important Elements of Good Dishes

COLOR

IN CHINA, A GOOD DISH MUST HAVE THREE ELEments: nice color, good aroma, and delicious flavor.

This means that each dish has the color it should have, and is cooked with other ingredients that make a pleasing combination of colors. For example, so-called red-cooked dishes, such as Shanghai duck and ham which is cooked with a large amount of soy sauce, should have a bright, reddish dark brown color. In China, red is the color for good luck and happiness, so although the color is closer to black, the dish may still be named red-cooked. Chinese speak of black tea as red tea. If the dish is cooked with light-colored white chicken meat which should be kept light, add only a little soy sauce or cook without it.

To make more colorful dishes for parties, we cook delicate green vegetables and red Smithfield ham with the light meat. Clear soup should be kept clear by using clear chicken broth or stock. Green and crisp vegetables should not be overcooked; thus they will retain their nice green color and good texture.

All cut ingredients should be cut uniformly. If one ingredient is shredded, all ingredients in that dish should be shredded; if sliced, all should be sliced, etc. Ginger and scallion should be

38

removed before serving, especially for party dishes. (But not to be removed from Shanghai duck and soy sauce fish which is cooked with a large amount of scallions.)

A good dish must have an appetizing aroma. The right kind and the right amount of spice and seasoning are important to make food smell good and to cover or neutralize the strong odors, but not to spoil the true flavor. Too much spice or poor choice spoils a whole dish.

AROMA

A good dish not only has a nice appearance and good aroma, but also has delicious flavor and interesting texture. Good, fresh ingredients, right seasoning, and right cooking period make dishes taste delicious and have good texture. The good cook's art is to bring out the good flavor in food by using the right cooking method, spice and seasoning, and the right preparation and decoration to improve the appearance, aroma, and flavor.

FLAVOR

Nowadays I feel that good dishes require not only the above three elements but also a fourth one — nutrition.

Food gives energy and it affects body health. Right diet improves health. Although fat and large amount of oil make cooking easy and give richer flavor, we know they are not very good for the heart, so I cut down on the use of fat and oil as much as possible in all my recipes. Lard gives clearer color and richer flavor, but it is animal fat. It is better to cook with vegetable oil. (See page 13 — cooking oil)

NUTRITION

In menu planning, we should think of serving a balanced diet; this means not too much meat or too many vegetables, not too rich or too light.

The Chinese manner of preparing vegetables is good nutrition practice; they are not overcooked, so they retain the full food value, without waste.

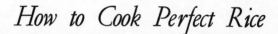

How to Cook Perfect Rice

I just cannot cook rice right. It never comes out well. I hear that complaint almost every time I talk about Chinese cooking with Americans. Rice is very important in Chinese meals; without rice it would not be a complete Chinese dinner. However, many Chinese do not eat rice at every meal in China. I put rice as the first lesson in my Chinese cooking classes, and every one is requested to cook it right. As I say, cooking is under our control, if we know why and how.

There are mainly two kinds of rice:

Long grain rice — The grains are long and narrow, absorb more water, and after cooking are fluffier. This is the only kind good for fried rice.

Short grain rice — The grains are short and wide and absorb less water. After cooking they are softer. Short grain rice is good for porridge or congee. In China, many people like soft rice, which is easier to digest. But most people, especially here, prefer drier and fluffier rice.

Raw rice needs just the right amount of water for cooking. Long grain rice needs more water than short grain rice. Cooked rice doubles in size and is translucent in color and soft to chew. Insufficient amount of water leaves inside of rice uncooked; it is still white and hard. Too much water, or more water than the rice can absorb, makes the outside of rice too soft and

40

mushy. The harder or softer all depends on how much water you put in. Rice recipes in many Chinese cookbooks make rice too soft.

Many people say: never stir rice or look at the rice while it is cooking. I think the reason is that they are fearful of breaking grains and of letting the steam escape while the cover is opened. I always like to tell my students to see and to smell food while they are cooking. This helps them to understand more about why and how. In case anything goes wrong there is time to save it. Everybody makes mistakes and only a good cook knows how to avoid and to remedy the error.

A gentle stir from the bottom up and around the edge before the water is all absorbed makes rice cook more evenly with less burning on the bottom. When you stir, some rice may stick on the pan edge. Scrape the grains down with the stirrer. A peek helps you to check whether there is enough water or not.

When the water is almost absorbed, the rice should be white and roughly double in size. Then cover it tightly, turn the heat very low and let it simmer for 20 to 30 minutes. The rice will turn translucent and soft. If the rice is still small, then it needs more water; 1/4 cup of hot water may be added at this time. When the water is absorbed the heat must be set very low, otherwise the rice will burn easily.

If the rice is cooked on an electric stove, the heat should be set very low before the water is absorbed. It takes about one minute on an electric stove to reach the degree of heat which is required.

Burned rice on the bottom of a pan is very hard to wash off. In case the rice gets burned a little bit, open the cover for one or two minutes. Then place a piece of bread on top of the rice. The bread will absorb a lot of smoky flavor and it works like a filter.

HOW TO STIR RICE WHILE COOKING

41

Sometimes the bread even turns a light brown. If the rice is burned quite a lot, then scoop out the unburned rice to another sauce pan, add ¼ cup of hot water, cover, and simmer again. Once rice is cooked it should not be kept too long before serving. If it must be kept, loosen the rice, with wooden fork or chopsticks, in a lifting motion very gently. Do not stir it. The rice should be kept in the same sauce pan until time to serve. Keep it warm over very, very low heat or in a warm oven. If there is to be a long wait, sprinkle a small amount of water around the edge, about two or three tablespoons.

Left-over cooked rice should be wrapped to keep it moist in refrigerator. Left-over cooked rice, if it is not soft, is especially good for cooking fried rice.

To warm up cold cooked rice, spread it on the top of newly cooked rice which is simmering (do not stir until the simmering process is through). Lumped cold cooked rice will be easier to separate by wet hands, or wait until it is warm to loosen it with a wooden fork or a pair of chopsticks. Keep rice warm in covered bowl for table serving.

Sometimes the rice, along the bottom and lower edge of pan, is usually formed into a layer which is stuck on the pan. The bottom part is browned. This layer of rice is called RICE SKIN in China. (We cook it with plenty of water to serve as porridge. If it is not very brown then separate it with wet hands to use as left-over rice.)

PLAIN
BOILED RICE

2 cups	**long grain rice** — about 1 lb.
2¼ cups	**water** — cold or hot

Wash rice 2 or 3 times, rubbing gently between the hands, and drain very well. Put rice and water into a sauce pan of at least 2 qt. capacity. Cover and bring to a boil over a medium high heat. As soon as it is boiling, turn heat to medium low and stir the rice with wooden spoon from the bottom up and around the edge. Scrape down the grains on the edge of pan. Cover and let boil slowly until water is absorbed. Stir gently once again and simmer over very low heat for 20 to 30 minutes. This makes 4 cups cooked rice. 4-6 servings.

Cook the rice as soon as the rice is washed. If short grain rice is used, reduce water to 2 cups.

Since you already know all the important information about rice, I am glad to offer you the following Chinese way in washing and measuring rice. Wash rice in the sauce pan to be used for cooking rice. Fill the pan with enough water to rub the rice between two palms. After a few rubbings, tip the pan gently to pour out the water from the pan. (The rice always settles to the bottom of the pan.) Wash the rice three or four times in the same way until the water becomes quite clear.

Now you start to measure the right amount of water by using your index finger as:

FIG. 1   First smooth the top of rice in the pan by using back of fingers. Then insert your index finger *straight* into the washed rice and touch the bottom lightly. Put your thumb on the side of index finger to mark the deepness of the rice, and keep the thumb in place until the water is measured.

Figure 1

FIG. 2   Now fill the pan with water (warm or cold) as deep as the rice. Then with the tip of index finger just touching the top of rice (not in the same hole when the rice was measured) add water until the level of water just reaches the tip of thumb. This means the rice and the water have the same depth in the pan. If you prefer harder rice use a bit less water. If short grained rice is used then reduce the water lower; if you prefer softer rice then fill the water over the tip of thumb.

To make the result successful you *must* follow these rules:

1. The pan must have uniform diameter. The upper and lower parts of the pan must be same width.

Figure 2

2. The index finger must be straight when measuring.

3. During the two measurings, the thumb must be kept in place.

4. After washing, the rice should be measured immediately.

When you follow this measuring method, you will be very happy not using a strainer, colander, or even measuring cup.

The old Chinese way, when rice is cooked in a WOCK, is to measure with the palm on the top of the rice. That way won't work in the ordinary sauce pan. The wock is wide at the top and narrow at the bottom. Also the size of hands is very different. Even the palm can not be fitted in the sauce pan.

All my students are happy to be able to cook perfect rice in all Chinese meals. They say now it is as easy as pie to make. Please read the above information carefully. Your rice has to be perfect!

Using Chopsticks The Proper Way

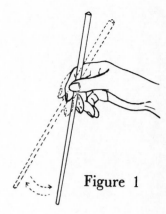

Figure 1

WHEN YOU EAT IN A CHINESE RESTAURANT, YOU may use a fork and knife as eating tools. But I think a pair of chopsticks can definitely give you a better and prouder feeling.

Chinese eating implements are customarily made of non-conductive materials such as ivory, wood, or bamboo. Because the Chinese dishes are served very hot, any metal tools may burn your mouth.

As a rule, the top end of the chopsticks is square and the bottom end round. Use the round ends to pick up food and carry it to your mouth.

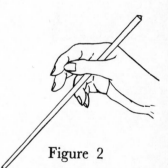

Figure 2

A pair of chopsticks looks so simple, so convenient, so peaceful. The following illustrations can tell you how to use the chopsticks in a proper way exactly as the Chinese do.

Figure 1. One of the pair is in an upper position.

Use thumb, index, and middle fingers to hold it. The right place to put your fingers is roughly at the middle of the chopsticks. (For children, it is advisable to hold it a little lower.)

The other chopstick is in a lower position.

Figure 2. Just rest the upper half of the chopstick on the juncture of your thumb and index finger, and the lower half on the end of the ring finger.

Figure 3. Together, they make a beautiful combination. Fix

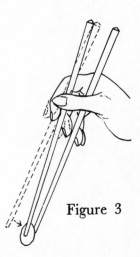

Figure 3

45

the lower one firmly and move the upper one freely as you wish. Your little finger is used to support the ring finger.

One thing you should not forget is that the two ends of the chopsticks must be even, and not crossed. Make them even by tapping the round ends on a plate or on your palm, which is in no sense bad manners.

To pick up rice from a plate is certainly not so easy. But it is not the Chinese way to serve rice on a plate. Instead we serve rice in a rice bowl. We do not pick up the grains of rice with chopsticks, but we gently shove them in our mouth directly from the bowl.

Usually Chinese people keep the square end of chopsticks clean to serve food to others.

When you hold chopsticks this way, at first you may be clumsy and slow. Don't be discouraged. Like any manual skill, it takes practice to manage well.

Tea

SERVING TEA IN CHINA IS QUITE DIFFERENT FROM in the United States. Tea has been the favorite drink of Chinese for centuries. It has developed into an important part of the Chinese culture. Men and women, adults and children, rich and poor, all drink tea instead of water. Scholars and poets love to get together in the gardens or mountains in beautiful scenery, to play chess or to compose poems. Tea is always served there. There are also many tea houses in the market section serving tea for vendors and coolies.

In China one of the jobs in the morning is to make a large pot of strong tea, which is diluted in the cup by adding hot water whenever needed. We keep the tea warm either by placing the pot in a tea-cozy or by burning a small piece of charcoal cake in the ash under the pot. We never serve tea with sugar and cream or milk.

Chinese tea experts pay attention not only to the varieties of tea, but also to utensils, water, and ways of boiling water. The water must be soft and fresh and just boiling a few seconds. Never over-boil. (Spring water is best, so at good resorts there is always a place beside the spring to serve tea.) Then pour the boiling water over the tea leaves immediately. The water is boiled only in a special kettle. In China the brass kettle is best. The stainless steel kettle will be most suitable here. We use chinaware,

47

glassware, or earthenware to brew and to serve tea. Metalware is supposed to spoil the flavor and the color of tea. The formal and old fashioned tea cup is a small chinaware bowl that opens wide at the top with a smaller lid set in the cup and a fitted saucer. The lid keeps the tea warm and also holds in the tea leaves while the drinker sips the tea, pushing the lid back. It is quite a technique to drink the tea from this kind of tea cup. Therefore we only use them on special occasions or on New Year's days. (We celebrate the New Year season as long as fifteen days.)

I divide tea into three main groups, namely: Jasmine tea, green tea, and black tea, which is called red tea in Chinese, as black is an unlucky symbol in China. (The tea leaves are black, but the prepared tea is red.) To enrich the fragrance, sometimes, we put certain kinds of flowers into certain kinds of tea. For instance, orange flower buds or chrysanthemums for green tea, and roses for black tea (red tea).

Whenever a guest drops in at the house or even in the office, a cup or a glass of hot tea is served. We rarely serve tea on the dining table as the Chinese restaurants in this country do. When guests leave the dining table a cup of hot tea is always served.

We never cook tea, unless a certain kind of tea is to be used for helping digestion. The proper way to make tea is to pour briskly boiling water over tea leaves. Use about 1 teaspoon of tea leaves to one cup of boiling water, and cover for 2 to 3 minutes before serving. When the first cup of tea is finished, another cup of boiling water may be added to the same tea leaves. If you make tea in a pot then the leftover tea leaves may be used to make a second pot of tea.

48

Differences Between
Home and Restaurant Cooking

RESTAURANT FOOD IS QUITE DIFFERENT FROM family food in way of handling. Standards of Chinese restaurants are remarkably different. High class restaurants, mostly, serve banquets. They also do catering by sending one chef, one helper and one waiter to the customer's home. Many restaurants have their own special dishes. Some of them only serve their specialties as afternoon or midnight snacks. Some famous old, old restaurants serve only one or two dishes, for which they are well known. They prepare only a certain amount and when that is sold out, as it always is, people who are waiting must come back the next day. They never care about the atmosphere of the dining room in which there are usually only a few unpainted tables and benches. These kinds of restaurants usually have their strange traditions or interesting family backgrounds or even fairy tale stories. Regardless of the poor atmosphere and service, customers still pour in, because the flavor of their dishes is incomparable.

Many dishes are profoundly loved. Because the ingredients are cheap, the appearance is not so nice, and the smell is very strong, they are rarely served in banquets but at small restaurants or at homes.

In China, restaurants use a large amount of charcoal as

49

fuel. Chinese restaurants in this country use large rings of gas which makes flame as high as 4-6 inches. They cut up the ingredients and set them in line next to stove, which is called a chop suey range. Some of the ingredients are half-cooked in advance. They start to cook when the order is placed. The dishes at the restaurants have more different ingredients in the same recipe. The restaurant can easily do this, as they serve a large number of people. Regular home dishes may use fewer items, but they have more true food flavor.

At home, the flame is much lower, but we have a definite time to serve and can concentrate on one meal, so the dishes at restaurant and home have their own good points. In other words, some dishes are better cooked at restaurants while other dishes are better cooked at home.

China is such a huge country with poor transportation facilities, that each province, even each big city, has developed its own way of cooking with the locally-produced ingredients. Chinese cooking can be divided into the following main schools, or styles:

PEKING or Mandarin

北京

PEKING STYLE OF COOKING is also named Mandarin style. Peking has been the location of the imperial palace for several centuries. As a rule, anything that is the best of its kind should be presented to the Palace, including the best food and the best chef. Peking is in the Northern part of China where the staple food is wheat flour. The imperial family liked the food made with flour too, even though it had its own rice paddy located outside the wall, west of Peking. Many famous Peking dishes are served with pancakes, such as Peking Duck and Moo Shi pork (see page 109 and page 129). They also have the best sweet and sour dishes, like Mandarin Pork (see page 134) and Mandarin Fish.

50

SHANGHAI style of cooking prevails in both the eastern and central parts of China. People there use more soy sauce and sugar in their dishes and serve rice at almost every meal. So, salty and gravy dishes are more suitable. They also have many dishes of fresh water fish and shellfish which are cooked alive or are cooked as soon as they are killed.

SHANGHAI

CANTONESE style of cooking prevails in the southern part of China. The Cantonese dishes at high class restaurants in China are very colorful. They use a large amount of pineapples and tomatoes to decorate the plate, and also use less soy sauce, to retain the pretty colors of the food. The Cantonese dishes in this country are very different because of limited labor. As you may have heard, there are no such things as American style chow mein and chop suey dishes in China.

CANTON

SZECHUAN style of cooking prevails in the southwestern part of China, including the famous city of Chungking. Because of the climate, people there like hot pepper very much as Mexicans do. Since World War II many American soldiers have come to enjoy the Szechuan dishes. Even now on Formosa (Taiwan) this kind of hot dish is also popular.

SZECHUAN

Recipes in this book are among the less fussy and most widely appreciated ones. I have selected from restaurant cooking and home cooking of different schools dishes which will be especially suitable to cook at home. I sincerely hope this book will bring joy to you, your family and your friends. Please read carefully before you start to cook.

51

How to Grow Bean Sprouts at Home

 BEAN SPROUTS ARE GROWN FROM DRIED MUNG beans, a kind of tiny green bean which Chinese call green beans. It is quite simple to grow perfect bean sprouts at home. The following rules explain how it should be done and give the reasons:

1. Mung beans need enough moisture to sprout. Too much water makes the bean rot; not enough water makes them too dry and they can not grow.

2. Plants need the right temperature to grow; the best temperature for growing bean sprouts is a room temperature of 68 to 75 degrees.

3. Plants need light for growing, but bean sprouts are an exception. Bean sprouts need a dark place to grow white and tender, so that the pot should be always covered. The best growing place is a dark corner of your basement. If you live in an apartment, you may use the kitchen closet or bathroom.

Although growing bean sprouts is quite easy, it involves careful timing. I suggest that you grow enough of them at a time to be used in several dishes or to share with your friends. Your youngsters will be delighted to grow bean sprouts for you. I think this is a good opportunity to give them some agricultural knowledge.

52

1. Soak 1 cup of dried mung beans obtainable in Chinese groceries in lukewarm water overnight. The soaked beans will almost double in size.

2. Cover the bottom hole of a *clean* 10"x8" (or bigger) clay flower pot with bathtub drain protector, rust-proof screen or cheese cloth to prevent the tiny beans slipping through the hole. Put the soaked beans into the pot. Water thoroughly at room temperature or under the faucet, then drain well. Cover the pot tightly and lift it into a large bowl to catch any drippings, or in basement basin or bath tub. The pot must be kept in a dark place and at room temperature. Water the beans in the same manner 3-4 times a day; you can omit watering at night. If the room temperature is quite high, water them more often.

3. Continue watering for 4 to 6 days but never disturb or stir the sprouts. You will see the beans gradually grow bigger and squeeze tighter into regular bean sprouts. In case the sprouts turn slightly red then water more often and with colder water — but not ice cold.

4. When the white and tender part of the top layer of bean sprouts reaches 1¼" in length (not counting the roots) they are ready. The middle and bottom parts of your pot of bean sprouts always grow faster than the top part, because there is more moisture and warmth. Now comes the most fun for you and your family. Pull the bean sprouts gently out of the pot into a basin with lots of water. Wash off most of/the green husks and part of the roots, stirring gently with your hands. Most of the husks settle at the very bottom of the basin with the cleaned sprouts on top of them. Some sprouts with husks and some empty husks will float on top of the water. Pick out the cleaned sprouts and drain well in a colander, or wash off the husks and roots by putting a small amount of sprouts into a deep-fryer wire basket. The holes of the basket should be large enough to let the husks and pieces of roots through, and the cleaned bean sprouts will

STEPS TO GROW BEAN SPROUTS

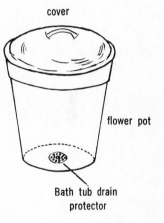

cover

flower pot

Bath tub drain protector

53

remain in the basket. Store well-drained sprouts (about 3 pounds or 12 cups tightly) in a plastic bag with holes and keep in the refrigerator, ready to use. Do not freeze fresh bean sprouts.

Chinese Table Dipping Sauces

IN CHINA WE USE MANY DIPPING SAUCES ON THE table for the dishes which are cooked without seasoning or not seasoned strong enough for individual tastes. To make your Chinese cooking complete it is necessary to list the major dipping sauces.

DUCK SAUCE

This is the dipping sauce well known to Americans. It is made of fruits and spices. There are two kinds available in Chinese groceries — imported and domestic. Sometimes the duck sauce is too thick or too sour to use. Then add some water and golden brown sugar to suit your taste. Blended chutney, peach or apricot preserve with some water may be used for a substitute, about 40% chutney, 40% preserve and 20% water. Lemon juice and golden brown sugar can be added to your taste.

MUSTARD SAUCE

This is a very strong, sharp and yellow-colored sauce. The colder the sauce the stronger it gets; it is better to make it a day ahead and store in the refrigerator (with a tight cover).

2 TBS mustard powder
4 TBS *cold* water
½ tsp vinegar
⅛ tsp salt

55

Mix the mustard powder with 1½ tbs water into a smooth paste. Add the remaining 2½ tbs water gradually and vinegar and salt making a smooth thin sauce. Cover the paste tightly and keep in refrigerator for later use.

HOI SIN SAUCE and OYSTER SAUCE

These sauces are very popular to serve as table dipping sauce in Cantonese food. About 1 to 3 tbs in a small dish on the table is usually sufficient. Sometimes the hoi sin sauce is garnished with ½ tsp of sesame seed oil. (See pages 14 and 21)

HOT PEPPER OIL

Fresh-made hot pepper oil has a wonderful appetizing aroma and with the red color it will delight the person who is fond of hot food.

1 TBS hot pepper flakes
2 TBS cooking oil
¼ tsp chili powder
⅛ tsp ground black pepper

Put the hot pepper flakes, chili powder and black pepper in a small heatproof bowl.

Heat the oil in a skillet or sauce pan. When the oil has started moving, drop a hot pepper flake to test. If the oil foams around the flake, then remove the oil immediately from the heat and pour over the flakes in the bowl. The oil should not be too hot or it will burn the flakes. The oil must be hot enough to foam in the bowl and give a sizzling sound to get the hot flavor out of the pepper flakes. It should have a red color.

Put on the table for individual use in dipping the food and garnish with noodles.

Some foods are cooked plain without flavor, so-called *white cooked,* such as Cold Cut Chicken (page 106), and everybody has a different taste in saltiness so a small dish of soy sauce is often served on the table for dipping. The soy sauce and sesame seed oil are the base and shredded or minced ginger root and/or scallion are added for more aroma and flavor. Sometimes crushed garlic is used as a substitute for ginger and scallion.

Soy sauce with sesame seed oil dipping:

¼ cup soy sauce

½ tsp sesame seed oil

Soy sauce with ginger and/or scallion dipping:

1-2 tsp ginger root and/or scallion (shredded or minced finely) added to above.

Soy sauce with garlic dipping:

1-2 garlic cloves (peeled and crushed) added to the soy sauce and sesame seed oil

Some people prefer to add a small amount of vinegar and sugar (golden brown is better) to the above dippings. You may do so to your taste.

SOY SAUCE DIPPINGS

This kind of dipping is served with seafood or salty pastries. You may serve with Fried Shrimp Chinese-style, Steamed Fish, or with steamed crabs.

¼ cup vinegar (**I** prefer cider vinegar)

1 TBS ginger root (shredded or minced finely)

Sometimes sugar and soy sauce are added when the dipping is served with steamed crabs. Sesame seed oil is *never* added.

VINEGAR AND GINGER DIPPING

This is roasted and ground Chinese pepper corn (page 20) with salt. It has a wonderful aroma and is only served with deep fried dishes (Shrimp Balls in this book). Since the oven is not

SALT AND PEPPER DRY DIPPING

57

common in China, and with such a small amount, we usually quick-stir them in a frying pan.

1 tsp Chinese pepper corn

2 TBS salt

Put the salt and pepper corn in a very small sauce pan. Heat the pan over medium heat and shake the pan constantly until you hear the crackling sound and smell the wonderful aroma. Shake for $\frac{1}{2}$ minute more and remove from heat, continuing to shake the pan for another $\frac{1}{2}$ minute (total about $1\frac{1}{2}$ to 2 minutes).

When the pepper corn is roasted and becomes crisp, then grind them in a mortar or put them on a piece of heavy paper and crush them finely with a rolling pin. It may be stored in a jar for future use. If Chinese pepper corn is not available then heat the salt and ground black pepper for a substitute.

Measurement

IT IS VERY HARD FOR AN AMERICAN TO PICK UP A Chinese recipe and cook it for the first time successfully. To meet the busy schedule and manage things just right, it is necessary to figure out how much work, time and money are involved in these dishes. As I said in the beginning, I wish you to have a good time in Chinese cooking. I have done my best to mention all the important information which is involved in cooking.

I list the main ingredients in weight and capacity for your shopping convenience. I also list the tablespoon as TBS and the teaspoon as tsp to avoid any confusion between them. All dried ingredients are measured dried before soaking, so there is no guessing and no soaked left-overs. I do not list the water which is not mixed with other ingredients to prevent any mistakes.

The measurements for salt and soy sauce are based on normal tastes and coloring. You may add a little more salt to suit your taste but not soy sauce. (With the variation of soy sauce it is even wise to *taste* every dish.) The combinations and the measurements of ingredients in the same dish are based on general traditions and the balance of the elements in a good dish and the convenience of buying. If you face an emergency or have something extra on hand, you may increase or decrease the amount of ingredients that is used or use other items for a substitute. Before you make any changes, be sure to check the amount of seasonings

59

and the cooking time. I always feel that Chinese cooking is so much like Chinese brush painting; you can use your own imagination to create a dish with concern to the *elements of a good dish* and the method of cooking. After all, cooking is an art.

The preparations are listed after the ingredients which must be prepared before starting to cook. (I do not list those ingredients which are simple to cut in preparation.) Sometimes in the middle of cooking, a beginner may find out that the next ingredient which is supposed to be added has not been washed, cut or softened.

I measured the cooking time with a stop watch, but cooking time is influenced by the thickness of pan, the heat, and the temperature of ingredients; therefore, I also mention the appearance of the ingredients at that stage for your double checking. Although I list the degrees of heat, the knob adjustments of gas stoves (even electric stoves) are not standard, the pressure of the gas is different, and sometimes the flame jumps itself.

For quick-stirring method, cooking is started with hot skillet. Such vegetables as pea pods, green peppers and bean sprouts should be crisp and should be removed from skillet as soon as the cooking is completed. Vegetables and beef are better a little undercooked than overcooked, as the heat will continue cooking them even as they are placed in serving plate.

For testing the tenderness of a large piece of simmered meat or a whole bird, pierce the heavy part of meat with a chopstick. If the chopstick can be pushed through easily and without blood coming out, that means the meat is cooked and tender. On smaller pieces of meat, touch with spoon or chopstick, and if the meat seems soft on the edges, and has cooked the right length of time, then it is done and tender. If the meat, especially large pieces, are at room temperature, it will take less time to be done or tender.

When you cook on an electric stove which cannot be adjusted instantly, you should turn to the degree which is desired about $\frac{1}{2}$

60

to 1 minute early. For quick-stirring cooking which does not give time to wait, then just simply lift on or off the skillet from the heat instead of turning switch. When the dish is just cooked, it may look dry and with too little gravy, but the amount of gravy will increase while serving.

In the table of contents each recipe is marked with the method of cooking and approximate timing; quick-stirring needs a short time but most of these recipes require last-minute cooking and serving at once. Simmering needs a longer time but most of these recipes can be kept warm or reheated until the time to serve. Quick-stirring with constant stirring means you have to be there. Simmering just needs turning occasionally and checking that the heat is not too high as the liquid will overflow in the pan. During simmering you could be doing other things.

Each recipe is also marked with inexpensive, moderately expensive, and expensive so you will have an idea which to pick and to match your pocket. As you may know, Chinese food generally is more reasonable than any other kind of food.

In an average Chinese family we always serve several dishes at one time for lunch or supper. With chopsticks (some families use serving chopsticks or spoons) everyone helps himself to suit his taste. A banquet never includes less than 10 dishes, which are served one at a time, and everyone around the table has his share from the dishes.

I want to make it clear that the number of servings from a Chinese recipe is very hard to tell. It depends on how many dishes will be served at the same time. To prevent confusion, I give two kinds of serving methods and numbers in my recipes:

1. American serving: means only one main dish is served along with soup, vegetables, or appetizer.

2. Chinese serving: means two or three main dishes are served at same time.

The quantity of the dishes is based on the convenience in

61

buying, cooking and serving. Some of the dishes can be kept nicely for a few days and reheated very well. With long cooking procedures, I then enlarge the amount for future servings.

You may double the recipes in this book to serve a larger group of people, but if you want to cook larger than double portions it is better to cook the dish twice because the size of pans and the amount of heat in the average family kitchen is not large enough for more than double portions.

In quick-stirring dishes use only one and one half times the amount of cooking oil when you double the recipe — especially with a well-seasoned, smooth skillet. In some dishes such as Sweet and Sour Pork or Shrimp, or Shrimp with Lobster Sauce the amount of water and cornstarch should be only one and one half times when you double the servings. This is because of the large amount of sauce in the single portions. Do not forget to use less salt and/or soy sauce when cutting down the sauces; one and one-half to one and two-thirds will be good, or to suit your taste.

The Measurements in this book:

TBS — tablespoon

tsp — teaspoon

1 TBS — 3 tsp

1 lb boned meat — 2 cups

A piece of sliced ginger root is about less than ¼″ thick and 1″ diameter.

All spoons and cups are level.

1 stalk scallion means the whole green and white.

Appetizers

IN CHINA WE SERVE COLD MEAT, SEAFOOD, AND vegetables to accompany the drinks before the main dishes. What to serve and how to serve depends on the people who are going to eat.

If it is a regular family meal, most of the time there is no appetizer; it is only served to the head of the family, with a little drink before the meal. The head usually is the grandfather or father. Women are not wine drinkers, and may drink only at parties or by doctor's advice to help blood circulation. The most simple dishes to go with drinks are spiced and roasted peanuts, sliced meats, and vegetables.

For a gathering of close friends, we generally serve tasty cold dishes such as chicken wings, pig's feet, etc., which are especially cooked to serve with drinks. The way of eating such dishes is not very graceful, but it takes a long time to eat, drink, and talk.

For a party there are always a few cold dishes which are served first with drinks. The dishes are cut neatly for easy eating and nice appearance. How many kinds of meat and vegetables are used in these dishes are determined by how fancy the party is. There are at least four items, but often eight, four kinds of meat and four kinds of vegetables. One kind of meat with one kind of vegetable is cut — normally sliced — and arranged nicely on a plate, placing the four plates in four corners of a round table.

Sometimes all the items are arranged beautifully on a large platter. The platter is placed in the center and passed around for serving. Everything on the plates or platter is cold. Combinations of different meats and vegetables depend more on the eye for color than the taste or flavor.

The appetizers listed in this book are suitable for serving at different occasions in this country.

In China egg rolls (spring rolls) are served as snacks. Here they are also good as appetizers, particularly for serving on the table. Whole pieces of Shrimp on Toast are also good to serve this way.

For serving to family and close friends, Barbecued Spare Ribs and Chicken Wings are excellent. As they are eaten with fingers, they should probably not be served at formal parties.

Shrimp Balls, Bacon-Wrapped Water Chestnuts, Seasoned Black Mushrooms, and cut small pieces of Shrimp on Toast are wonderful. Cut pieces of Pork Strips or Tea Eggs are good for hors d'oeuvres at cocktail parties. Do not serve big pieces of food at such affairs without using a fork and plate, as the fillings or the pieces of food may fall out. The food should also be quite dry without dripping.

Pork Strips and Fried Wonton are good for all occasions and nice to serve on the plate at the table and also may be picked up with the fingers.

Hot appetizers (most deep fried) should be served *hot*. Those listed in this book, except Pork Strips, may be kept warm in a low oven for a short period — about $1/2$ hour. The best way is to place them on a rack over a baking pan so the oil will not stay in the food. (The same applies to re-heating.)

24 pcs **water chestnuts** — fresh or 1 small can
2 TBS **light brown sugar**
8 strips **bacon** — regular length or 12 short strips

1. Drain canned water chestnuts very dry and mix with sugar. If fresh water chestnuts are used, then wash, peel and rinse.

2. Cut bacon into 3 sections (if short bacon then cut in half).

3. Wrap bacon around water chestnut and attach both ends with a round toothpick. If the bacon seems too short then stretch it slightly. This preparation can be done hours ahead.

Roast wrapped water chestnuts in baking pan in hot oven — 425° — for about 15 minutes or until bacon is golden brown. Serve hot.

If you are waiting for guests, then roast in a medium oven, or light brown them and keep warm in a very low oven.

This is a good Hors d'Oeuvre and is especially suitable for cocktail parties or unexpected friends, as canned water chestnuts and bacon are easily kept on hand.

Although bacon is not Chinese, the water chestnut can give you a feeling that this is indeed Chinese. Fresh water chestnut is sweeter and crisper but must be peeled and is expensive. See page 8 about water chestnuts.

SEASONED	2 cups	**black mushrooms** — dried
BLACK	2 TBS	**cooking oil**
MUSHROOMS	2 TBS	**soy sauce**
	2 tsp	**sugar**
	¼ tsp	**M.S.G.**
	1 tsp	**ginger root** — minced or juiced, as desired

紅
燒
冬
菇

1. Soak black mushrooms in 3 or 4 cups boiling water and cover for 15 minutes. Then trim off stems, squeeze out water, and cut the mushrooms into even bite-sizes (large ones into 4, medium ones into 2).

2. Mix soy sauce, sugar, M.S.G. and ginger juice (if used) in a bowl and set aside.

Put oil in a hot skillet over medium high heat. Add mushrooms and spread them out on the bottom of skillet. Turn and brown both sides. Then stir in minced ginger root (if used). After a few stirrings, turn heat lower and pour the soy sauce mixture over the mushrooms. Stir until the mushrooms absorb the soy sauce evenly. Serve hot, warm or cold, as a side dish, or pierce with toothpicks as an hors d'oeuvre.

This is a wonderful side dish, an easy hors d'oeuvre, and the cost is low, too. In this dish, the mushrooms are brought out to the best of their texture and flavor. They can be kept nicely in the refrigerator for a few days. Whoever likes black mushrooms will be so pleased with this recipe. Bamboo shoots may be added.

2 lb	**chicken wings** — about 10 pcs.	
½ cup	**cooking oil**	
1 slice	**ginger root**	
1 tsp	**dry sherry**	
2½ TBS	**soy sauce**	
3 TBS	**oyster sauce**	
1 tsp	**sugar**	

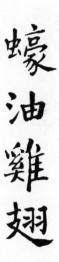

*CHICKEN
WINGS
WITH
OYSTER
SAUCE*

Scald the wings in boiling water as on page 31, and singe the pinfeathers. Pat the wings dry with paper towels. Cut the joints of the wing into three sections, and discard the wing tip section.

Put the oil into a deep skillet or Dutch oven over medium high heat. Add ginger root and half of wings to the skillet and gently brown both sides. Remove the browned wings and brown the rest of the wings in the same manner. As the oil tends to splatter, it is safer to remove the skillet from the heat about one minute for the turning and removing of the wings. You may also wear gloves. After the wings are browned, drain off the oil which is in the skillet. Add the wings, sherry, soy sauce, oyster sauce, and sugar into the same skillet. Pour in one cup of water. Bring to a boil. Simmer with cover on for 10 minutes and baste the wings for another 10 minutes without cover, turning occasionally, or until a half cup of liquid remains. Serve hot or cold. It is not necessary to re-heat left-overs.

EGG ROLLS

½ lb	**good hamburger**
1 tsp	**sherry**
½ TBS	**corn starch**
¼ tsp	**black pepper**
1 TBS	**golden brown sugar**
1 TBS	**brown gravy syrup**
2 TBS	**cooking oil** (in which to cook the filling)
3½ tsp	**salt**
few slices	**ginger root**
¼ lb	**celery** — shredded
¼ lb	**onion** — shredded
1½ lb	**cabbage** — shredded
2 TBS	**flour**
½ tsp	**M.S.G.**
1 lb	**raw bean sprouts** — 4 cups packed tightly
18 pcs	**egg roll skin** (about 1 lb)
1	**egg** — beaten with 2 TBS cold water — Use to brush the edges to seal egg rolls.
1-2 qt	**cooking oil** for deep frying egg rolls

春捲

For Filling

Mix hamburger with sherry, corn starch, pepper, sugar and brown gravy syrup in a large bowl.

Place oil in a large sauce pan over medium heat. Add salt and ginger then the celery and onion, and cook about 3 minutes. Add mixed hamburger to skillet, stirring constantly and separate the hamburger into fine pieces. When beef is cooked, place mixture in colander and drain off excess liquid into a pan. Spread meat mixture out flat and let cool. Discard ginger slices.

Return drained liquid to the same sauce pan over

68

medium high heat and cook cabbage until transparent and soft (not all at once, for it would overflow the pan; but little by little as you can fit it into the pan). Stir constantly. Again drain off liquid through colander by pressing. Mix drained cabbage with flour and M.S.G. powder and set aside to cool. (Both the cabbage and the beef mixtures may now be kept in the refrigerator until it is convenient to make and fry egg rolls. The filling should never be used while warm.)

When it is time to make and fry rolls:

Mix cabbage, beef, and bean sprouts together and crush the bean sprouts lightly by hand. Place about ⅓ cup or a good scoop of mixture in an egg roll skin; fold it up neatly (see illustrations on next page). Deep fry the folded egg rolls in oil at 350° to 375° immediately until golden brown. Place browned egg rolls on end in colander to drain off oil. Serve hot. (Makes about 18 egg rolls.)

The egg roll skin will not puff if the oil is not hot.

If for later serving, then place on rack to cool. Never pile up warm egg rolls; the brown and crisp wrapping will turn soft.

This is the exact filling used in the egg rolls which I made especially for the schools. This is not authentic. Chinese egg roll is called "Spring Roll" which symbolizes the coming of Spring. We serve them during the New Year holidays or as a snack in the afternoon. The Spring Roll is smaller-sized with thinner skin, and beef is never used for filling as the beef is not common in China.

If you are living in a city with a Chinatown, then it is much easier to use machine-made egg roll skins which are sold in Chinese noodle factory in 5-lb packages. If they

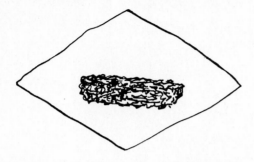

FIG. 1 Put about 1/3 or ¼ cup of filling in center of egg roll skin.

FIG. 2 Fold over filling one edge of egg roll skin.

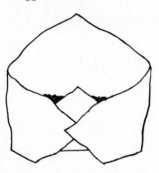

FIG. 3 Fold over other two edges and make like an envelope with one edge still open.

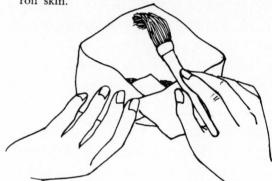

FIG. 4 Brush open edge with egg and water mixture.

FIG. 5 To seal, start rolling up from bottom of envelope very neatly and tightly making sure all filling is sealed securely; if it isn't then it will burst open in the oil and make a big mess.

70

do not want to separate the package for you, then keep the unused portion in freezer wrapped in separate smaller packages for future use in making egg rolls or wonton. Defrost the egg roll skin thoroughly before use.

If you are making the egg roll skin at home (See page 199), then use less filling, about ¼ cup, because the home made egg roll skins are smaller and softer. Since they are softer it is more important to deep fry them as soon as they are wrapped.

The best way to fry is to wrap a few egg rolls, enough to fit in pan, and fry them while wrapping the others.

Since there is quite a procedure to making egg rolls, I suggest making enough to please your family and your friends. Left-over egg rolls can be kept in the refrigerator for 2 or 3 days, or in a freezer. (Only the bean sprouts will lose their good texture.) Reheat them in a covered skillet over very low heat for 20 minutes and turn them once, halfway through heating — 40 minutes for frozen egg rolls. For large amounts, reheat in oven.

PORK STRIPS
Restaurant Style

2 lb		**fresh pork tenderloin meat,** or 2 pcs. lean meat *eye* from pork butts (see page 214).
1½ TBS		**soy sauce**
2½ TBS		**Hoi Sin Sauce** (see page 21)
1 TBS		**dry sherry**
⅛ tsp		**Chinese five spices powder or garlic powder** (see page 23)
¼ tsp		**red food coloring** (if desired)
½ TBS		**sugar** or 1 TBS honey

1. Trim fat and gristle from meat.
2. Mix soy sauce, Hoi Sin sauce, sherry, Chinese five spices powder, food coloring and sugar
3. Rub the pieces with the above mixture. Set aside for at least one hour.

Put pieces on a rack in a roasting pan containing 1½-2 cups of water and roast slowly at 300° for 2 hours or until done. Do not let meat touch the water. Add more hot water if necessary to keep the bottom of the pan covered during cooking. When halfway through cooking, brush meat with mixture, then turn it over brushing the other side with remaining mixture. Serve hot.

Slice on the table or in the kitchen.

Many Americans asked me how to cook pork strips tender and juicy as at restaurants. The above recipe will give you that result. Because pork strips are all lean meat, overcooking will make them dry and tough, yet it *is* pork and should be cooked well done. The long period roasting in the oven with a low heat and the steam from the water in the roasting pan will do the job right.

The best time to serve pork strips is as soon as they are cooked. Reheat left-overs in low oven, wrapped in aluminum foil. (The red color will fade but they will remain juicy.)

Cut cooked pork strips into bite-size cubes. Pierced with round toothpicks, they make wonderful hors d'oeuvres. Duck sauce and mustard are served as dipping. Leftover pork strips are good to cook with Fried Rice, Egg Foo Yung, or added to Bean Sprout Salad.

In China, especially Southern China, wonton is very popular both at home and at restaurants. To fold wonton, you need plenty of leisure hours, so the way of folding at restaurants is much rougher than family style. I shall tell you the proper family way of folding wonton. (See page 201)

There are three ways to serve wonton:

1. Fried wonton as an appetizer
2. Wonton soup (page 86)
3. Boiled wonton as a whole meal

Wonton Filling I (raw before folding)

½ lb	**ground pork**
1 TBS	**soy sauce**
1 TBS	**oil or dripping**
2 TBS	**water or stock**
¼ tsp	**salt**
¼ tsp	**M.S.G.**
1 tsp	**finely minced scallion**
1 tsp	**corn starch**
1 tsp	**pale dry sherry**
¼ cup	**finely chopped shrimp** or fine-flaked crabmeat may be added

Mix all the ingredients in a large bowl and set aside until ready to use.

FRIED WONTON

炸
餛
飩

73

Wonton Filling II (pre-cooked before folding)

½ lb	**ground pork**
½ TBS	**corn starch**
1 TBS	**soy sauce**
1 tsp	**pale dry sherry**
1 TBS	**oil**
½ tsp	**salt**
¼ tsp	**M.S.G.**
2 TBS	**minced black mushrooms** (if desired)
2 TBS	**minced bamboo shoots** (if desired)
1 tsp	**minced scallion**

Mix ground pork with corn starch, soy sauce and sherry.

Put 1 TBS oil in heated skillet and stir in the pork mixture until the pork is cooked (about 2 minutes). Then add the remaining ingredients and put into a large bowl. Mix well and set to cool.

FIG. 1   Put ½ teaspoonful of the filling in the center of the wonton skin. Support the skin on the fingers of both hands with your two thumbs in the top center.

FIG. 2   Now fold the outside edge even with the inner edge by using your thumbs and two index fingers.

FIG. 3   Using both thumbs, press the wonton skin firmly around the filling.

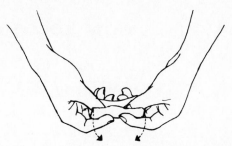

FIG. 4   Now make a fold with the filling at the center, using the two thumbs to hold the fold and to keep the skin firmly pressed around the filling.

FIG. 5   The fold you have just made will form two wings on either side of the filling. Now fold these two wings together backwards.

FIG. 6   Wet the corners of these two wings with water or egg whites, overlap, and press them firmly together between your right thumb and index finger (left thumb and index finger if you are left-handed).

FIG. 7   Now you have a completed wonton as you can see.

All of the students in my cooking classes know how to fold wonton in this manner. You may be slow in beginning but you will speed up later and enjoy it forever. Even your children will enjoy making wonton with you.

See next page for cooking wonton.

HOW TO COOK WONTON:

Deep fried — Deep fry wonton in hot oil, 350° for raw filling; 375° for cooked filling, until golden brown. Serve hot with duck sauce and mustard sauce. (page 55)

Boiled — Put wonton gently in a large sauce pan with enough boiling water, allowing the wontons to swim freely, over medium heat. Cover and bring to a boil. As soon as the water boils add ½ cup cold water for cooked filling and 1 cup for raw filling. When the water is boiling again then remove sauce pan from heat and let the wontons remain in water for 5 minutes with cover on. Drain well to serve dry on plate or add in the soup (page 86).

Wonton skin is obtainable at Chinese noodle factory in Chinatown. I rather like to use regular sized egg roll skin and cut it into four even squares. If you are not near a Chinatown, see page 199 for How to Make Wonton Skin.

Ready-made skin can be kept nicely for days in the refrigerator. If you freeze them, be sure to thaw them out thoroughly before use.

To serve at a large cocktail party, fried wonton is much better than egg rolls. With meat or vegetable filling inside, wonton is neatly wrapped by wonton skin. They are bite-sized and you can use your fingers, no need for fork and plate.

Deep fry wonton beforehand and keep warm in the oven. Leftovers may be kept in freezer and reheated in a baking pan (450°) for 15 minutes without defrosting.

Fry wonton in deep oil over medium heat until golden brown. Serve as an appetizer or hors d'oeuvre with or without duck sauce or mustard.

To serve wonton as an appetizer, I favor using Wonton Filling II, because it sometimes happens to beginners that the outside skin is already dark brown while the inside meat is still not well done. It is safer to use cooked filling, then you don't have to worry about the meat. You have to only watch to see if the outside skin is turning to a pretty golden brown.

2 lb	**chicken wings** — about 10-12 pcs.	*CHICKEN*
⅓ cup	**soy sauce**	*WINGS*
2 TBS	**sugar**	*SHANGHAI*
1 TBS	**dry sherry**	*STYLE*
2 slices	**ginger root**	
few cloves	**star anise**	

紅
燒
雞
翅

Sear and scald the chicken wings in boiling water and singe the pinfeathers over a high flame. Rinse and drain.

Put the cleaned chicken wings and the rest of the ingredients with ⅓ cup water into a large sauce pan or Dutch oven. Bring to a boil and simmer with cover for 20 minutes. Stir occasionally while simmering. Baste the wings without cover for 15 minutes until about ½ cup liquid remains. Spoon liquid on wings and stir frequently for darker, even color. Serve hot or cold.

Many Americans drink liquor without any food, but the Chinese are different. They have several dishes that they serve with drinks, among which chicken wings and duck wings are the most popular in informal parties. In Shanghai, duck wings made an obscure snack store very famous.

Chicken wings cooked this way (duck wings, too) are better served cold. Cook the day before and keep them overnight.

The most popular giblets dish is also cooked in this manner. 3 or 4 TBS oyster sauce may be added if you want, but then reduce soy sauce to ¼ cup.

SHRIMP ON TOAST

2 strips	**bacon** — 3 strips if it is short
1 lb	**raw shrimp** — shelled and deveined
5	**water chestnuts** — minced; if you use fresh water chestnuts — peeled and minced. Or ¼ cup minced celery.
1 tsp	**dry sherry**
¼ tsp	**M.S.G.**
1 tsp	**salt**
10 slices	**white bread** — day old is better
3-4 cups	**cooking oil** for deep frying, enough to fill skillet at least 1″ deep.

1. Grind bacon with shrimp into a paste.

2. Mix the ground shrimp and bacon in a bowl with water chestnuts, sherry, M.S.G. and salt. Set aside.

3. Cut crusts from bread. To have the bread in uniform pieces, use a cardboard pattern to suit the size of bread. Shake off crumbs, if any.

4. Divide the mixed shrimp paste into 10 parts, one part on each slice of bread and spread it evenly. To prevent stickiness, dip your knife into cold water before spreading. Spread surface should be completely smooth with neatly covered edges (not the sides) and corners.

Pour oil to the depth of 1 inch in a skillet over medium high heat. When oil is hot — about 350° — test the oil by putting a small piece of bread crust in the oil. If the oil foams along the crust, it means the oil is hot enough for frying. Fry bread shrimp side down until edges are brown. (Be sure the bread is floating freely). Then turn to brown the other side. Drain on paper. Serve hot.

This is a dish which is good to serve on all occasions. In China, it is usually served at banquets; here, we serve it as an appetizer. It is wonderful to serve at cocktail parties for hors d'oeuvres. Cut fried bread into small pieces (triangles or oblongs) by a gentle sawing motion for neat edges, and pierce the small pieces with toothpicks. Paprika and minced parsley may be used to decorate the pieces. (Or add 1 tbs minced parsley to the shrimp paste.)

Shrimp paste may be prepared the day before and spread on bread hours ahead; they even can be fried early and kept warm in the oven.

If there are left-overs they may be kept in the freezer and reheated in a medium oven.

TEA EGGS

12 to 18	**eggs** — medium or small size
3 TBS	**black tea** or 6 TBS used tea leaves
3 TBS	**soy sauce**
2 TBS	**salt**
1 TBS	**star anise cloves**

茶
葉
蛋

1. Hard boil the eggs about 25 minutes starting in cold water over medium flame.
2. Cool eggs in cold water for few minutes and make cracks on the shells by rolling them firmly on the table.

Put the cracked eggs and all the ingredients in a large sauce pan or heavy pot. Add enough water to cover. Cook and simmer for 1 hour or more. Serve hot or cold.

Never shell the eggs before serving. The shell keeps them moist. The cracks on the egg shells make a beautiful design on egg whites like the cracks on antique porcelain.

This is a popular picnic item in China and it is wonderful for hors d'oeuvres here. It is served both by rich families and can be bought at street corners, especially in Hangchow, where vendors put the eggs in a small wock (Chinese frying pan) which is kept warm over a small wood flame.

Tea eggs can be kept nicely with the liquid in the refrigerator several days.

SHRIMP	2 strips	**bacon** — 3 strips if too short
BALLS	1 lb	*raw* **shrimp**
	5	**water chestnuts** — finely minced; if fresh water chestnuts, then peeled and minced.
	1 tsp	**dry sherry**
	¼ tsp	**M.S.G.**
	½ tsp	**salt**
	3-4 cups	**cooking oil**

1. Rinse shrimps, shell and devein.

2. Grind bacon with shrimp twice through the blade with the smallest holes, making a smooth paste.

3. Mix the shrimp paste with minced water chestnuts, sherry, M.S.G. and salt in a mixing bowl. Set aside.

4. Have ready a small bowl of cold water, a cup or more.

Heat oil in a small sauce pan, enough to fill the pan at least 1¼" deep at 350° over medium heat.

Dip two teaspoons in cold water. Spoon a teaspoonful of shrimp paste and toss it between two spoons for smooth surface and round ball shape. Then carefully slip the ball into the oil.

Continue to make other balls in same manner, about 10 at a time, depending on the size of the pan. The balls should not be too crowded to allow for stirring and even browning. When the balls are floating and puffed to a bigger size and light brown, remove to colander and drain off the oil. Spread them on kitchen paper towel, or keep warm in oven. Serve hot or pierced with toothpicks for hors d'oeuvres.

Shrimp balls are very good for hors d'oeuvres at formal cocktail parties. For a neat and nice appearance the balls should be even-sized and have a smooth surface. As shrimp paste tends to be sticky, dip the spoons in cold water before spooning paste to prevent stickiness and make the surface smooth. You may make the balls smaller or larger but must have enough deepness of oil to float the balls.

After removing from oil the balls may shrink but the flavor remains the same. One tbs fine minced parsley may be added to the shrimp paste for decoration and more flavor.

---

2 pieces	**fresh spare ribs** (each about 2 lbs.)	
3 TBS	**soy sauce**	
5 TBS	**Hoi Sin sauce** (see page 21)	
2 TBS	**pale dry sherry**	
¼ tsp	**Chinese five spices power or garlic powder** (see page 23)	
½ tsp	**red food coloring** (if desired)	
1 TBS	**sugar**	

BARBECUED SPARE RIBS

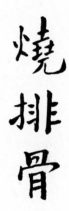

1. Trim fat and gristle from ribs. Cut off soft bone ends and slash through about 1½ inches between thicker ends of bones for more flavor and even cooking.

2. Mix soy sauce, Hoi Sin sauce, sherry, Chinese five spices powder, food coloring and sugar in a large bowl.

3. Rub the pieces with the above mixture. Set aside for at least one hour.

Put pieces on a rack in a roasting pan containing 1½-2 cups of water and roast slowly at 350° for 50 minutes or until done. Do not let ribs touch the water. Add more hot water if necessary to keep the bottom of the pan covered during cooking. When halfway through cooking, brush ribs with mixture, then turn them over brushing the other side with remaining mixture. When ribs are cooked, remove the water from pan and turn oven up to 450° and brown both sides (about 15 minutes). Cut into strips between the bones and serve with or without duck sauce and mustard sauce.

In China the barbecued spare ribs are not as red as the barbecued spare ribs served in the Chinese restaurants here. If you would like to have them as served in the restaurants, just add ½ tsp red food coloring to the sauce mixture (strawberry red shade is more attractive). The sugar and five spices powder you may add or omit according to your taste.

For outdoor barbecuing, roast ribs in kitchen oven at 350° first, then brown over outdoor grills. The ribs can be roasted days ahead.

My experience is that children and even adults love to do the browning themselves. In this case, cut ribs into wide strips (2 ribs to a strip) before final browning to prevent their falling through the grill into the fire.

The soft bone ends can be cooked with spare ribs for your family members who like to nibble in the kitchen, or use the trimmed lean meat for other dishes which require sliced, shredded or ground pork.

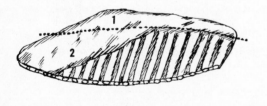

A   B

Cut off 1 as shown then trim 2 off. Then cut through 1½ inches—2 inches as shown in B.

82

Soup

SERVING SOUP IN CHINA IS DIFFERENT THAN HERE in America. In most parts of China we serve soup during the family meal with other dishes. For banquets there are normally two soups; one of them is served in the middle of the courses, the other one, usually with whole duck or chicken, at the end with a few heavy dishes which are accompanied by rice. Most Chinese like to mix the rice with soup in their own rice bowls. The Cantonese serve soup before other main dishes. They like to have a very large bowl of soup with enough for everybody to have a second or even third serving. At our home, we use individual soup bowls beside our rice bowls at the same time on the table. It is because we drink soup instead of water or milk.

Tasty soup depends on good stock or chicken broth. Good clear chicken broth is so useful in Chinese cooking. Many good chefs use clear chicken broth instead of water for cooking. I have enjoyed very much the convenience of using the canned chicken broth in this country. When I use it in soup, I prefer to dilute it with an equal part of water. First, it is more economical; second, I do not want the strong flavor of broth covering flavors of other ingredients. If you can get live-killed fowl easily, then follow the method on next page for making chicken broth. If you have chicken, duck carcass or pork bones, etc., then make the stock yourself. Chicken broth and stock should be as clear as possible.

83

In serving soup it is very easy to stretch the amount to serve unexpected friends just by adding water, stock, or chicken broth, but do not forget to add a little salt. If you use water then add some M.S.G. (⅛ tsp).

Another convenience of serving soup is that most soups can be prepared partly until the time to serve. Only Mandarin cucumber soup should be served as soon as the cucumbers are added. If you have to wait, then do not put the cucumber in until serving time. The Wonton soup, as the Mandarin cucumber soup, should be served as soon as the wonton is cooked, but you can keep the wonton out of the soup until it is ready to serve. In thick soups the corn starch should be added to the soup at the time of serving. This also applies to eggs. Bean threads in Meat Balls soup have to be added at the last minute, also.

Ham with Winter Melon soup can never be over-cooked. The job of adding ingredients at the last moment is very easy, and you can enjoy the extra cooking time by preparing something else, or wait for guests who are late for dinner.

CHICKEN BROTH

1	**fowl** — live killed is the best
1 TBS	**dry sherry**
2 slices	**ginger root**
1 stalk	**scallion**

Scald and sear the bird by method on page 31, and store two pieces of fat from the lower cavity for other uses.

Put the fowl and all other ingredients in a large pot with enough water to cover. Bring to a boil. Turn heat down *immediately* to a simmer. Spoon off residue on the liquid as clean as possible. Simmer until tender — about 1½ to 2 hours. Serve the broth alone as a soup with salt garnished with scallions, or cook it with other ingredients for a different soup. Serve the cooked fowl hot or cold with soy sauce dippings (see page 57).

Clear tasty broth depends upon good and long simmering. Skim off the fat which may be used to cook vegetables like Chinese cabbage or spinach (page 169 and 173). I like to cut off the white meat (breast) before cooking the bird. Fowl is quite tough but the white meat is tender for quick-stirring dishes such as Chicken with Green Pepper, etc.

Cook the pork bones, bird carcass with enough water to cover them. Add 1 slice ginger root, 1 tsp dry sherry and bring to a boil. Simmer for 1 to 2 hours and skim off fat and residue.

Beef and lamb bones are not suitable in making stock for Chinese soup as they have a very strong flavor.

STOCK

白
湯

------

1 can	**chicken broth** — or 2 chicken bouillon cubes with 2 cups warm water — or 2 cups stock with 1 tsp salt
2 cups	**water or stock**
1 tsp	**salt**
1 thin slice	**ginger root** — if obtainable
½ tsp	**dry sherry**
2	**eggs**
1 TBS	**scallion** — minced or fine shreds
¼ tsp	**M.S.G.** (if bouillon or stock is used)

EGG DROP SOUP

SERVES 4-6

木
樨
湯

Beat eggs slightly with dry sherry.

Mix the chicken broth, water, salt, and ginger slice in a sauce pan. Bring to a boil and remove ginger slice. Stir beaten eggs into boiling soup. Remove from heat instantly. Garnish with minced scallion. Serve hot. If chicken broth is not used, add ¼ tsp M.S.G. to soup.

85

If you prefer thicker soup, stir in corn starch mixture — 2 tbs corn starch in ½ cup cold water — before adding the eggs. The desired shape of egg drop is obtained by the speed of stirring when you pour egg into the boiling soup. If you want to make big pieces of egg drop, you just stir the soup slowly. On the other hand, if you want to make finer pieces of egg drop, stir the soup quickly.

After learning how to make this soup, many students of my cooking classes like to drop eggs into almost any kind of canned soup at home.

WONTON SOUP

SERVES 4-6

餛
飩
湯

1 can	**chicken broth** or 4 cups of stock and ¼ tsp M.S.G.
1 tsp	**soy sauce** — optional. Replace with ¼ tsp salt
½ tsp	**salt**
1-2 doz	**folded wontons** (see pages 74-75 and 201)
1 TBS	**scallion** — minced
¼ cup	**egg garnish** — optional (see page 164)

Put chicken broth, soy sauce, salt, and 2 cups of water in a medium sauce pan and bring to a boil. Set aside. If 4 cups of stock is used, then omit the 2 cups of water.

Put cooked (see page 76) and drained wontons in individual bowls or a large serving bowl. Pour the boiling chicken broth over the wontons and garnish with scallion and egg shreds. Serve immediately.

In Southern China we serve wonton as a whole meal either at a small party or a big festival celebration. In my home town, we often serve wonton for Sunday dinners or holiday lunches. We rarely deep fry wonton but cook them in boiling water. We then serve them in soup or drain them out and put them on a plate, using vinegar or soy sauce as dipping.

We like to pan-fry the left-over cooked wonton as you do your home-fried potatoes. Left-over wontons should be drained and separated on a plate for cooling before storing in refrigerator.

2	**very small, thin cucumbers,** or 1 medium size	
¼ cup	**lean pork** — thin sliced	
2 tsp	**soy sauce**	
½ tsp	**dry sherry**	
1 tsp	**corn starch**	
1 can	**chicken broth** — with 2½ cups water or 4 cups stock with 1 tsp salt	
1 tsp	**sesame seed oil**	

MANDARIN CUCUMBER SOUP

SERVES 4-6

黄
瓜
湯

Peel cucumbers, leaving some green underskin. Split down the middle, hollow out and discard the seedy portion. Cut crosswise diagonally in ¼ inch slices, making 1½-2 cups.

Mix pork slices with soy sauce, sherry, and corn starch in a bowl and set aside.

Heat chicken broth with water or stock in a sauce pan and bring to a boil. Stir in pork mixture until the soup boils again. Then add cucumber slices. After two or three stirs remove from heat, garnish with sesame seed oil, and serve immediately.

This soup is famous in Peking. The fresh aroma, crispness, and greenness of the cucumber depend on fast cooking and the prompt serving of the soup. Never, never overcook them, and serve the soup as soon as the cucumber is added. Maybe the cucumber will seem too raw to you, but by the time you are through serving, it will be just right to eat.

Near Peking there is a small town, Feng-tai 豐 台 It once served as a greenhouse to the Palace. It not only grew flowers, but also supplied vegetables in winter.

I can remember seeing from the train window, as I passed by Feng-tai in the winter, many vendors selling cucumbers on the platform. The cucumbers were about six inches long and packed in small woven trays. They were quite expensive, and since most people could not afford to buy enough to make a dish for all members of the sizeable Chinese family, the best way was to make a soup and let everyone have a share.

In warm weather farmers sell freshly picked small cucumbers especially for use in this soup.

In this country, it is better to select the fresh, thin, tender ones when you buy cucumbers from the market. If you grow cucumbers in your own vegetable garden, you can pick them when they are young. Wash cucumbers with sponge and slice them. Do not throw away the seeds or peel the skin. (Of course, the seeds are not even formed.)

CHINESE	¼ cup	**dried shrimp**
CELERY	1 small head	**Chinese celery cabbage** (about 1 lb)
CABBAGE	⅛ lb (2 oz.)	**dried bean thread**
AND	1 tsp	**dry sherry**
DRIED	2 TBS	**cooking oil**
SHRIMP	1½ tsp	**salt**
SOUP	2 slices	**ginger root**
SERVES 4-8	1 can	**chicken broth** (about 2 cups)
	4 cups	**water or stock**
	½ tsp	**M.S.G.**

1. Soak dried shrimp in sherry with 3 TBS water.
2. Discard the tough outside leaves of cabbage and cut cabbage into 1½-inch chunks.

88

3. Soak bean thread in warm water until soft, then cut into shorter lengths, 6-8 inches. Rinse and drain.

Heat oil in a large sauce pan or pot. Add salt, ginger slices and cabbage chunks. Stir and cook until cabbage is wilted. Put in all the ingredients except bean thread. Bring to a boil. Cover and simmer until cabbage is transparent and tender. Add bean thread. When soup is boiling again, remove from heat, add M.S.G. and serve immediately. (Do not put bean thread in soup too long before serving).

This soup is often served with moo shi pork and pancakes for a whole meal. As the pancake is dry, so we need the soup to accompany it. If you serve this soup in the same manner, then be sure to make enough as people often need a second or third serving.

Pork or Smithfield ham may be substituted for dried shrimp. Fresh shrimp is not suitable in this soup.

蝦米白菜湯

MEAT BALLS AND BEAN THREAD SOUP (CHINESE VERMICELLI)

SERVES 4-6

1 cup	**ground pork**	— ground beef may be used
1 TBS	**soy sauce**	
½ tsp	**dry sherry**	
¼ tsp	**M.S.G.**	
½ TBS	**corn starch**	
1 tsp	**salt**	
1 can	**chicken broth**	(about 2 cups)
⅛ lb	**bean thread**	

1. Mix meat, soy sauce, sherry, M.S.G., corn starch, and ¼ tsp salt in a mixing bowl.

2. Soak bean thread in warm water until soft, then cut into shorter lengths, 6 to 8 inches. Rinse and drain.

Put chicken broth, the remaining ¾ tsp salt and 3 cups of water in sauce pan. Bring to a boil over medium heat. Form the mixed meat into balls (size of golf balls) between two soup spoons. Dip spoons in boiling broth each time for easy forming and smooth surface. Drop the balls in the boiling broth one by one until the mixed meat is finished. Cover and simmer for 10 minutes. Add the softened thread, stir a little, and serve immediately.

You may cook the meatballs first and keep warm, when it is time to serve add the bean thread. Then it should be served immediately.

1 lb   **winter melon**
¼ lb   **Smithfield ham** —cooked or uncooked—sliced
1 can   **chicken broth** (about 2 cups)
1 slice **ginger root** — if available

1. Peel the green skin off the melon. Discard the seeds and cut off the soft part next to seeds. Wash, drain and cut into about ½-inch thick by 2-inch long slices.

2. Cut off skin and black surface of ham, if any, then slice.

Cook the sliced winter melon with 2 cups of water in a sauce pan. Bring to a boil. Boil slowly over low heat for 20 to 30 minutes until the melon is translucent and tender. Add ham, chicken broth and ginger. Cook for another 10 minutes. Serve hot.

Winter melon must be cooked tender and soft. It almost never can be over-cooked. This soup can be kept warm in the sauce pan over very, very low heat till time to serve, and also re-heated very well.

Sliced pork may be used as a substitute for ham, then ½ tsp salt should be added.

Old cucumbers can be substituted for winter melon but take less time to be cooked tender.

*PEKING
HOT AND
SOUR SOUP
(THICK
SOUP)*

SERVES 4-6

酸
辣
湯

¼ cup	**pork** — shredded
1 tsp	**dry sherry**
3 TBS	**corn starch**
1 can	**chicken broth** with 1½ cup water or 3½ cup stock with 1 tsp salt.
½ tsp	**salt**
1 TBS	**soy sauce**
¼ cup	**dried wood ears** — black fungus
¼ cup	**dried golden needles**
½ cup	**bean curd** — shredded — about ½ small cake
¼ tsp	**M.S.G.**
1	**egg** — beaten
2 TBS	**cider vinegar**
¼ tsp	**white ground pepper**
1 tsp	**sesame seed oil** — for garnishing
1 TBS	**scallion** — minced — for garnishing

1. Mix the shredded pork with sherry and 1 tsp corn starch (out of the 3 TBS).

2. Soak wood ears and golden needles in separate bowls with boiling water (each about 2 cups). Cover and soak for 15 minutes.

Snap off wood pieces from wood ears and hard stems from golden needles, if any. Cut golden needles in halves and break the large pieces of wood ears into smaller pieces. Wash, drain, and squeeze out water.

3. Mix the remaining corn starch (2 TBS and 2 tsp) with ½ cup cold water.

4. Put the vinegar and pepper into a large serving bowl.

92

Put chicken broth with 1½ cups water (or stock), salt and soy sauce into a medium sauce pan. Bring to a boil and stir in the mixed pork. After boiling for 1 minute, add wood ears and golden needles. Again boil for another minute. Add bean curd and M.S.G. As soon as the soup is boiling again, stir in the well-stirred corn starch mixture until it thickens. Mix in beaten egg and remove from heat immediately. Pour the soup in the serving bowl with the vinegar and pepper. Garnish with sesame seed oil and scallion. Serve hot.

This soup has no snob appeal. It is very popular but is never served at big banquets because the ingredients are very inexpensive in China.

In our restaurant this is the best-known soup. I was very much surprised when I found so many Americans liked it. One customer even ordered it to take out to his New Jersey-bound plane.

CRAB AND BEAN CURD SOUP (THICK SOUP)

SERVES 4-6

蟹
粉
豆
腐
湯

½ cup	**crab meat** or 1-3¼ oz. can — flaked and soft bones removed
2 TBS	**oil**
2 tsp	**salt**
1 slice	**ginger root**
1 tsp	**sherry**
⅓ bag	**spinach** — washed and chopped
1 can	**chicken broth** (13¾ oz.) with 2 cups water or 4 cups stock and 1 tsp salt
1 cup	**bean curd** — diced — about 1 small cake
3 TBS	**corn starch**
½ tsp	**M.S.G.**
1	**egg** — beaten

Mix corn starch with ½ cup of cold water.

Put oil into sauce pan (at least 2 qt. capacity), add salt, ginger slice, crab meat, sherry, and spinach. Cook and stir until spinach is wilted. Add chicken broth with water or stock. Bring to a boil, put in bean curd, then stir in the corn starch mixture and M.S.G. As soon as the soup is boiling again, stir in beaten egg and remove from heat immediately. Serve hot.

In China, we use fresh water crabmeat in this soup but it is not available here. The canned crabmeat gives quite a good result and is easier, too. If you cook this soup on Fridays or fish days, you may use water instead of chicken broth or stock.

Poultry

CHICKEN IS THE MOST COMMON AND DELICIOUS meat all over the world. How to cook the chicken is according to the age and the parts of the chicken.

FOWL It is the most elderly chicken and therefore the only bird good for chicken broth. Breasts are good to use in Chicken Velvet or any quick stirring cooking with small pieces of chicken meat. Wings and legs are used in cooking Empress Chicken (page 107) and Chicken Wings (page 67) but need longer simmering to be tender.

YOUNG ROOSTER, CAPON, AND PULLET These are most suitable to use in all the dishes in this book. Breasts and thighs are only used in quick-stirring cooking. The wings and legs, especially the drumsticks, have more gristle and skin and so they are not suitable for dishes which call for chicken meat.

FRYER (OR BROILER) This is only good to cook with the bone as it is very tender. Just cook it long enough to be well done but be careful not to over-cook it as the meat will fall from the bone.

Chicken meat (as other meat) should be cooked tender and juicy to preserve the best of chicken flavor. If the chicken is cooked with bones it should be tender but not fall from the bone.

95

In China we use the best of the parts of the bird to cook into a few different dishes. First, there are no chicken parts available in the Chinese market. We buy live chickens and kill them at home. Second, the different parts of chicken meat are at their best in certain ways of cooking. Most Chinese do not like simmered or long-cooked white meat as it will be dry, but it is so good if cooked in quick-stirring method or Chinese deep fry. Especially the white color is very pretty.

Since many Chinese dishes use certain parts of meat in certain dishes, preparation of the chicken is essential, especially in the country where no chicken parts are available in the market. If you can buy live-killed chicken—young rooster, capon, or pullet are suitable—it is worth the trouble preparing chicken in the following manner and having the best flavor in chicken.

Also, I feel very strongly it is my duty to help you to be independent and serve the best of dishes.

PREPARING A CHICKEN
(You need a sharp firm knife)

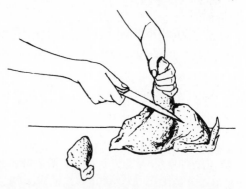

FIG. 1   Lay the chicken on its back. Cut through at the first joint between the drumstick and thigh bones and remove the two drumsticks. This joint is located at the first bend from the tip of the leg.

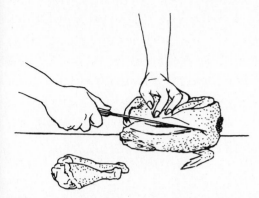

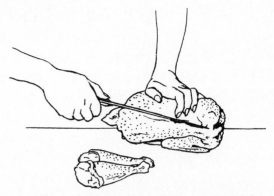

FIG. 2   Now roll the chicken over on its side. Cut through the skin in front close along the breast-bone down the length of the chicken.

FIG. 3   Now turn the chicken over. Make a cut through the skin down the center of the backbone along the whole length to the tail.

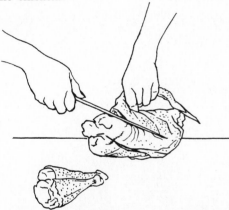

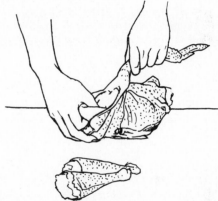

FIG. 4   Grasp the wing in your left hand (right hand, if you are left handed) and find the wing joint between the two bumps on the chicken's shoulder. Cut through the skin and gristle and sever the joint, but leave the wing attached as shown in Fig. 5.

FIG. 5   Hold the body firmly through the hole just cut (the hole is located inside of the shoulder bone which makes a sharp angle) and with a hard pull draw the wing toward the tail. The wing and the outside layer of breast will then come off in one piece.

97

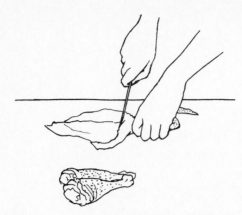

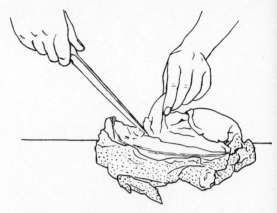

FIG. 6 Lay the piece skin down. Now sever the wing from the breast from the breast meat by holding the wing in your left hand, and cutting through the meat and gristle but not skin at the end of the wing. Push the breast meat away from you. Cut off the skin at the end of wing and discard. Trim the fat and membrane, if any, off the breast meat.

FIG. 7 Next to the breast bone you will find left a strip of white meat attached to a piece of gristle close to the neck. With the point of your knife sever and lift up this gristle. Separate the white meat from the breast bone and pull it off.

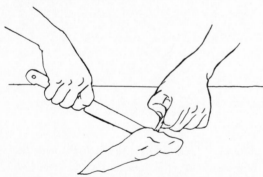

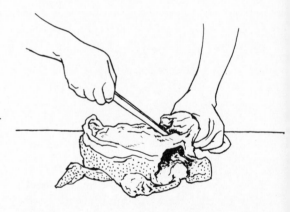

FIG. 8 Lay the breast meat flat and hold the tip of gristle with your fingers. Push the meat away enough so that you can get a good grasp on the gristle. Then holding the meat with the edge of the knife, pull the gristle free.

If you buy just the breast part of the chicken use the same method for removing the gristle.

FIG. 9 Now take the second joint of the leg in your left hand. Pull it back and lift its inner end to expose the joint. Cut off the leg - thigh - through the tendons at the joint and separate the meat from the leg bone to free the leg meat. Trim away the gristle and fat.

Turn the chicken over and do the same thing for the other side. Trim off the good meat left on the body, to use it for the recipes requiring small pieces.

Now the chicken is in parts:

The carcass and leg bones to be simmered for stock.

The drumsticks and the wings for Empress Chicken (page 107), Curry Chicken (page 104) and Chicken wings (page 67), or to use in your American dishes.

The meat from breast and thighs to use for Chicken with Green Pepper (page 100), Chicken with Mushrooms (page 101). The white and breast meat for Chicken Velvet (page 102), or to use as you wish.

Since in China we have to kill the chicken at home, it is not hard to save the blood which should be diluted with salt water and steamed. This is a delicacy and often cooked with Peking Hot and Sour soup, but never goes on the banquet table.

Generally, duck is cooked whole and served whole. Pulling duck's feathers is quite a job in China, but with the frozen duck here it is almost free from feathers, only the small feathers around the tail, under the wings and legs need to be cleaned off. (The same with chickens).

Chicken and duck feet, duck's tongue, and the glands from the rooster and male duck (cooked with soups) are among the delicacies often served at banquets.

Shreds of cooked chicken and duck are torn by the hands along the grain rather than cut by knife. First, they are tender and will be messy if cut across the grain; second, the fingers can reach to the corners of the carcass.

CHICKEN WITH GREEN PEPPERS

SERVINGS:
CHINESE 5-6
AMERICAN 2-3

青椒雞丁

2 cups	**chicken meat, diced** — 2 whole breasts or breasts and thighs of one 3-lb chicken.
3 tsp	**corn starch**
1 tsp	**dry sherry**
¼ tsp	**M.S.G.**
2 tsp	**salt**
4 TBS	**cooking oil**
1 clove	**garlic** — peeled and crushed
½ cup	**bamboo shoots** — diced
½ cup	**water chestnuts** — diced
2 medium	**green pepper** — diced. Rinse before cut

1. Bone and skin chicken and remove all tendons and gristle (See pg. 98, fig. 8). Then dice the meat.

2. Mix chicken meat with 1 tsp corn starch, sherry, M.S.G., and salt. Set aside.

3. Make a mixture of the remaining 2 tsp corn starch in 5 TBS cold water and set aside also.

Pour oil into hot skillet over medium high heat. Add garlic, then stir in the mixed chicken meat. Stir constantly until almost done, about 2 minutes. A stiff spatula makes a good stirring tool as the chicken meat tends to stick to the pan. Add water chestnuts and bamboo shoots, stirring for 1 minute, then mix in green pepper thoroughly. Put in well-stirred corn starch mixture, stirring for a few seconds until gravy thickens. Remove from heat and serve immediately.

You may replace green pepper with pea pods — cut them crosswise in 3 or 4 sections — if so desired. No matter which one you use, you must keep them green and crisp.

One of the ladies in my cooking class once served this dish to some thirty guests.

She cooked chicken and other ingredients a day ahead and left green pepper to be cooked while reheating the chicken at the time of serving. That was the right way to keep green pepper crisp and green in this dish for a large party.

2	**chicken breasts** (whole) or 1 large
1 tsp	**dry sherry**
2 tsp	**corn starch**
1½ tsp	**salt**
¼ tsp	**M.S.G.**
1 can	**French mushrooms** — 4 oz. canned and sliced
1 cup	**pea pods** or ½ cup parboiled or frozen green peas
2 slice	**ginger root**
4 TBS	**cooking oil**

CHICKEN WITH MUSHROOM

SERVINGS:
CHINESE 5-6
AMERICAN 2-3

1. Bone and skin the chicken breast. Trim off membrane and fat. Cut the meat into thin slices. The tip of the breast is very thin, so for splitting that part into even slices see page 98.

2. Mix the sliced chicken with sherry, 1 tsp corn starch, 1 tsp salt and M.S.G. in a bowl.

3. Drain the mushrooms over a bowl and save the liquid.

4. Mix the remaining 1 tsp corn starch with the liquid from the mushrooms.

5. String pea pods, rinse and pat dry with kitchen towel.

Put the oil in a hot skillet over medium high heat. Add ginger slices and chicken. Stir constantly for less than

101

2 minutes until the chicken meat turns white. Drain the chicken in a small colander or strainer over a bowl. Discard ginger slices. Return the oil from the bowl to the same skillet over medium heat. Add the drained mushrooms and the remaining ½ tsp salt. After a few stirrings add the pea pods and continue stirring constantly until the pea pods turn to darker green. Mix in the well-stirred corn starch and cooked chicken meat. When the liquid thickens, serve immediately.

This dish is pretty and delicious for any occasion. It is very much like Chicken Velvet but easier in preparing and cooking. Of course, Chicken Velvet is more tender and juicy. Thin-sliced cooked Smithfield ham may be added for more color and flavor. Also, ¼ cup roasted almonds may be used as a garnish.

CHICKEN VELVET

SERVINGS:
CHINESE 5-6
AMERICAN 2-3

½ lb	*white* **chicken meat** — about one breast (both sides)
3	**egg whites** — medium sized egg
1 cup	**chicken broth** — or cold water
½ tsp	**dry sherry**
½ tsp	**salt**
¼ tsp	**M.S.G.**
1 TBS	**corn starch**
2 cups	**cooking oil** — for frying

1. Remove the skin and 2 pieces big gristle (page 98, fig. 8) of chicken breast. Dice chicken meat.

2. Blend diced chicken meat in blender at low speed, adding chicken broth or water a teaspoon at a time. When chicken becomes a thin, smooth paste, remove the paste into a mixing bowl and discard the gristle which is attached to the blades.

102

3. Fold in the slightly beaten egg whites, remaining chicken broth, sherry, salt, M.S.G. and corn starch with the chicken paste.

Heat oil in skillet over medium heat to about 300° Spread the thin chicken paste into the oil by the tablespoonfuls. The oil will cover it; then immediately add another layer, and another or two. When the chicken paste turns white and firm, *not brown,* immediately remove skillet from heat and put the cooked chicken paste into colander or strainer. Drain off the oil.

INGREDIENTS FOR COOKING STEP 2

2 TBS	**Virginia ham** — cooked and minced (optional)
1 cup	**snow peas** — stringed, rinsed and dried — about ⅛ lb. (or green peas, parboiled or frozen).
2 TBS	**cooking oil** — or oil in which chicken paste was cooked.
¼ tsp	**salt**
½ TBS	**corn starch**
¾ cup	**chicken broth or water.** If water is used, then increase salt to ½ tsp.

Mix the corn starch with chicken broth, or water, and set aside.

Heat oil in the same empty skillet which was used to cook chicken, over a medium high heat. Add salt and stir in snow peas for a few seconds. Add in the well-stirred cornstarch mixture, stirring constantly. As soon as the liquid thickens, fold in cooked chicken very gently, remove to a serving plate and garnish with minced ham. Serve immediately.

This is a very delicate dish, especially attractive in color. You will be proud to serve it. In this country, only a few Chinese chefs can cook this dish exactly as the best chefs in China do. My students and I have tried many times to simplify the process of preparing by using the electric blender instead of grinding, or the old Chinese method of chopping. In this dish, the smoother the chicken paste, the better.

If the electric blender is not available, then use either of the following methods to make the chicken into paste:

Method 1: Using a hand grinder, grind the diced chicken meat three times through the metal blade with the smallest holes. After the chicken is very smoothly ground, then mix it very well with other ingredients. (Discard the gristle which sticks to the cutting blades.)

Method 2: Old Chinese chopping way: Chop the diced chicken very, very fine on a hardwood cutting board. Turn the bottom side up every so often for even chopping; sprinkle 1 TBS chicken broth or water from the 1 cup which is required in recipe to avoid stickiness on the knife. (Do not sprinkle more than 1/3 cup). When the chicken is chopped very smooth, blend very well with other ingredients. Discard the gristle which is chopped into the wooden board.

CURRY CHICKEN

SERVINGS:
CHINESE 6
AMERICAN 4

加厘雞

1	**chicken** — fryer — about 2½ lb
1 cup	**onion** — sliced
2½ TBS	**curry powder** — prepared curry paste is better, but not easy to obtain.
1 TBS	**chili powder**
4 TBS	**cooking oil**
1½ tsp	**salt**
½ tsp	**M.S.G.**
2½ TBS	**flour**

104

1. Scald chicken in boiling water and pull feathers and singe pinfeathers. Cut the chicken into big chunks about 20 pcs. Try to cut the wings and legs through the joint for fewer pieces of bone.

2. Mix curry and chili powder into paste in ½ cup of water.

3. Mix flour smoothly with ½ cup of water.

Put oil in a large heavy pan (the enameled pot is best) over medium high heat. Add onion and stir frequently until light brown. Mix the curry paste for a few stirrings and add the chicken pieces. Stir for 2 minutes until the chicken is evenly coated with curry. Pour 1 cup water and bring to a boil. Cover and simmer over very low heat for 20 minutes. Add salt and M.S.G., then remove the cooked chicken to a serving casserole or deep plate.

Stir the flour mixture smoothly in the pan to thicken the gravy. Pour the gravy over the chicken and serve hot. (Or keep warm in low oven until the time to serve.)

This is not exactly an authentic Chinese dish. I learned to cook this dish from an Indian friend. Curry can improve your appetite and is wonderful to serve with rice. Be sure to cook plenty of rice. In this dish, chicken can be replaced by beef (the kind of beef for stewing). You should then increase the simmering period to 1 hour or more until the beef is tender and increase the water from 1 cup to 1½ cups.

If curry paste is used then omit chili powder.

COLD CUT CHICKEN

SERVINGS:
CHINESE 8
AMERICAN 4

1		**chicken** (3 to 5 lb) — live killed pullet is best.
1 TBS		**dry sherry**
3 slices		**ginger root**
1 stalk		**scallion**

白切雞

Sear and scald the bird in boiling water. Pull out any remaining small feathers and singe pinfeathers. Rinse and drain. In a very large pot have enough water to cover the bird. The best way is to put the bird in the pot, measure the water, then take the bird out.

Boil the water in the pot over high heat. When the water is boiling, plunge the bird in the water and let water cover the *whole* bird. Add sherry, ginger and scallion. Turn off the heat before the water boils again. Cover the pot very tightly and let stay for one hour. Turn on the heat again and watch to turn it off before the water boils again. And set aside for another 1 hour. Pierce a chopstick through the thigh of the bird and then pull out. If there is no blood from the hole then the bird is cooked. Otherwise repeat the third time of heating in the same manner. Let the bird stay for another ½ hour and drain off water. Place the bird on large plate and serve *cold;* or keep in refrigerator to serve the next day.

The meat of the bird is tender, juicy and delicious but not flavored with seasoning, so we serve it with soy sauce dipping (see page 57). Do not use strong-flavored sauce as it may spoil the light and good flavor of the bird.

In China we chop the bird in pieces before serving on the table. Chopping chicken with bones is not an easy job, and with the small pieces of bones it is not convenient to eat. I suggest you carve it, as you do roasted chicken, before or at the table.

My husband, Thomas, was once in a streetcar in Shanghai and overheard two women talking about how to make good cold cut chicken. He got some ideas from their talking, and therefore I was able to improve my technique in making this dish based on the new information. The soaking in hot water (not boiling water) makes the chicken juicy and tender. Meanwhile, the flavor of the chicken remains and is not lost in the water.

4	**chicken wings**
4	**chicken legs**
½ cup	**soy sauce**
2 cups	**water or stock**
1 TBS	**sugar**
few cloves	**star anise**
2 slices	**ginger root**
1 TBS	**dry sherry**
1	**scallion**
1 cup	**black mushrooms** — dried
1½ cups	**bamboo shoots** —in chunks
1 tsp	**salt**

EMPRESS CHICKEN

SERVINGS:
CHINESE 6-8
AMERICAN 4

1. Chop chicken wings and legs into big chunks, and sear and scald in boiling water. Rinse and drain well.

2. Fold whole scallion into 2″ or 3″ length and tie together with thread.

3. Pour boiling water over black mushrooms, cover, and soak for 15 minutes or more until soft.

Put the chicken and all other ingredients into a large sauce pan or Dutch oven. Cover and bring to a boil, then simmer for ½ hour or until tender. Stir occasionally to prevent sticking to pan. Baste over medium heat for 10 minutes to reduce liquid and give even color and flavor. Remove scallion and serve hot or warm. This dish may be placed in a warm oven until ready to serve or cooked a day ahead.

CHICKEN LIVERS WITH PEA PODS

SERVINGS:
CHINESE 4-6
AMERICAN 2-6

½ lb	**chicken livers** — about 1½ cups
1 tsp	**dry sherry**
¼ tsp	**M.S.G.**
3 TBS	**soy sauce**
3 tsp	**corn starch**
4 TBS	**cooking oil**
¼ tsp	**salt**
1 slice	**ginger root** — if desired
¼ lb	**snow peas**

雪豆雞肝

1. Trim membrane off chicken livers and cut diagonally in ½-inch thick slices.

2. Mix 1 tsp corn starch, sherry, M.S.G., 1 TBS soy sauce with the chicken livers and set aside.

3. Mix the remaining 2 tsp corn starch, 2 TBS soy sauce and ¼ cup water in another bowl. Also set aside.

4. Remove stems and strings from snow peas. Rinse in cold water and pat dry with a towel.

Put 2 TBS oil and ¼ tsp salt in hot skillet over high heat. Add ginger slice and pea pods and cook not more than 1 minute, stirring constantly. Remove pea pods and spread them out on a plate. (Discard the ginger slice).

In the same skillet, adding the remaining 2 TBS oil, cook chicken livers over high heat about 3 minutes. Stir constantly until no more blood comes out. Add well-stirred corn starch and soy sauce mixture, then pea pods. Stir a few seconds until gravy thickens. Serve immediately.

In China, the most expensive chicken part is giblets. Whenever we cook chicken, the gizzard is saved for the important or favorite person of the family, or sliced in several pieces so each one can have a share. It is quite impossible to train most Americans to like gizzard, so I just use chicken livers.

For duck:

1	**large duck,** the larger the better
1 cup	**dry sherry**
½ tsp	**brown gravy syrup**
1 TBS	**corn syrup** — such as Karo syrup
⅛ tsp	**red food coloring**

Serve with Pancakes, one of the sauces, and Scallions

For Pancakes:

1 ¾ cups	**flour**
¾ cup	**boiling water**
1 tsp	**sesame seed oil** or cooking oil (see page 21)

For Sauce No. 1 —

¼ cup	**Hoi Sin Sauce**
2 TBS	**Soy Sauce**
1 tsp	**sesame seed oil**

For Sauce No. 2 —

¼ cup	**Japanese dark miso**
1 TBS	**soy sauce**
1 TBS	**golden brown sugar**
1 tsp	**sesame seed oil**
1-2 bunches	**scallions**

北京烤鴨

Defrost duck thoroughly. Scald the duck in a large pot with enough boiling water to cover the duck. Let the duck soak for 5 minutes, then rinse it in lukewarm water. Pull out small feather roots with a tweezer and cut off the tip two sections of the wings. Save the giblets, neck and wing tips to make soup with the duck carcass later.

109

Dry the duck inside and out with a kitchen towel and place in a large oval deep plate which will be fitted to the duck. Pour the sherry over the duck and let stay in the sherry for one hour, turning occasionally for even soaking.

Remove the duck and mix the brown gravy syrup, corn syrup and the red coloring in the plate with the remaining sherry.

Rub and turn the duck in the sherry mixture for even coloring about one minute.

Bend a heavy wire (about 10″ long) and make two hooks at the ends. Hook the duck through the tail end and be sure it is strong enough to hold the whole duck. Use a chopstick to stretch the wing ends apart from the body. Hang the duck in the air with the hook at the other end and place a dish or bowl to catch the drippings.

Use a portable electric fan to dry the duck for at least 4 hours or more. Turn around for even dryness.

Use the metal stick from the rotisserie on your stove to hold the duck and place on the holding tray to roast in a low oven (300°) for 1½ hours. Wrap the wings and legs and the opening of neck and stomach edges with aluminum foil to prevent those places from burning.

Remove the duck to the rotisserie and empty the duck fat which is in the bottom of rotisserie holding tray (do not remove the foil yet) and set the duck turning over a medium low heat for ½ hour on rotisserie. Remove the foil at the last 10 minutes and serve immediately.

While the duck is drying and roasting, you may start to make the pancakes and prepare the scallions and sauce

110

which are served with Peking Duck.

Pancakes — see page 203.

No. 1 Sauce — Mix ¼ cup Hoi Sin sauce with 2 TBS soy sauce and put into two small dishes for convenience of quick serving. Garnish with ½ tsp sesame seed oil in each dish.

No. 2 Sauce — Authentic sauce for Peking Duck is prepared with Fava bean paste. The following is the closest to it.

¼ cup	**Japanese dark miso**
1 TBS	**soy sauce**
1 TBS	**golden brown sugar**
1 tsp	**sesame seed oil**

Mix the above ingredients together with 2 TBS or more cold water (depending on the thickness of the miso) into a smooth thin paste. Place in two small dishes and garnish with ½ tsp sesame seed oil in each dish.

Scallion — Remove the roots including the hard tips and then cut the white part of scallions in 3" long sections. (The green tops are not used in this recipe.) Split both ends of the sections with several ½" deep cuts, and soak the sections in cold water and store in refrigerator for 1 to 2 hours. By then the ends will open as flowers. Drain off water and place in two small dishes or place around in the sauce dishes, and serve on the table.

When you start to serve the duck you and all the people must be seated for the serving. Holding the duck on the metal stick upright, first carve the crisp skin in 2 or 3-inch square pieces from the breast, back and thighs, serving these first with Mandarin pancakes. Next, the meat is served.

The duck is not seasoned so the sauce is needed to flavor it. First, open the pancake on the individual plate (clean plate is essential) and spread about 1 tsp of the sauce on the pancake. Then put 1 or 2 pieces of skin or meat with it, with or without scallion, and roll up and eat at once.

The carcass is good to make stock for soup, especially Chinese Celery Cabbage soup (page 88), omitting the dried shrimp.

This is the world renowned duck from Peking, China. It is often served at banquets. The best Peking duck is served in special restaurants in Peking. The chef's helper brings a few prepared ducks to let you make your choice. When you have made the decision then they will start to cook.

Serve the skin first with pancakes, then the meat. The small pieces of meat which are left on the carcass is quick-stirring cooked with bean sprouts. Iron pot grilled egg yolks with duck fat is like Mandarin Eggs (page 159), and the carcass is used for making Chinese Celery Cabbage soup. One duck usually serves 4 to 6 persons for whole meal.

The ducks in Peking are especially bred to be cooked in this way. When the ducks are full grown (about 10 lb.) they are put individually in small cages which just fit the duck. The duck has no room to walk around and is forced to feed on a kind of grain mixture in small rolls the size of a large frankfurter. The duck becomes big and fat in a short period.

When the duck is killed, scald it and clean it very well. Leave the whole head intact, then remove the inside intestines very carefully through the bottom small hole. All this procedure is very gently done so as not to break any of the skin. Tie the neck with a string and pump air from the bottom small hole so the skin is puffed up and separates from the meat. Plug the hole so that no air can escape. Now hang the duck in a cool and airy place for a day or two to dry the skin. The weather in Peking most of the time is cold and dry, so it is best fitted for preparing this kind of duck.

112

Peking duck is a restaurant dish and never prepared at home. Since it is so famous, many of my friends asked me to put the recipe in this book so more people could enjoy this wonderful dish.

With frozen duck the neck is cut off and the opening at the bottom is so big it is impossible to pump air in the duck. Also the duck is much smaller. It is impossible to reach the same results as with the duck in Peking. All the time I worked on this recipe I tried very hard to reach the best results with the easiest procedures. (This is the only hard dish in this book.) I want to delight the people who have been in Peking and had this duck before, and also the people who have never heard of it.

The following is a must in serving:

You must hold the duck in the air on the rotisserie stick and cut skin, placing the pieces crisp side up and spread out on a plate. The skin will not be crisp (which is the best part of it) if it is covered, so the people should not wait for you but eat as soon as possible. It is better to use two dishes of sauce and scallion to be passed from opposite ends so as to speed the serving.

If you do not have a rotisserie on your stove, then try using a roasting turkey rack to hold the duck up and place over a baking pan to catch the drippings of duck fat. After 1½ hours of roasting at 300°, remove the duck fat from the baking pan and then roast for another ½ hour at 375°. Hold the duck straight up when carving the skin.

The weak point of roasting duck in a high oven is the greasy smoke which comes from the duck dripping in the baking pan being heated from the bottom. It is not like the heat of a rotisserie which is from two sides or the top, and the convenience of using the metal stick holds the duck in roasting and carving. It is also nice to do the last higher heat roasting in an outdoor rotisserie.

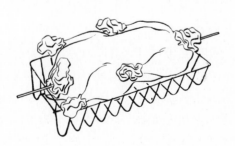

SHANGHAI DUCK

SERVINGS:
CHINESE 6-8
AMERICAN 3-4

1	**duckling** — about 4-5 lbs
1 bunch	**scallions** — cut into 3 sections
2 slices	**ginger root** — if available
several cloves	**star anise**
½ cup	**sugar** — or less — to your taste
1 TBS	**dry sherry**
¾ cup	**soy sauce**

Defrost duckling if frozen. Remove and discard any large pieces of fat from the cavity. Soak duckling and giblets in boiling water for several minutes until skin shrinks. Pick out feathers with fingers or tweezers, then rinse.

Put scallions, ginger slices, anise cloves and giblets in bottom of a heavy oval pot or Dutch oven. Then put duckling in, breast side down, and pour sugar, sherry, soy sauce and ½ cup of water over all. Cover tightly, bring to a boil, and simmer 1½ to 2 hours or until tender. If the cover of the pan is not very tight, then add ½ cup more water.

When approximately half done, turn duckling breast side up. It is done — tender — if a chopstick is easily pierced through the thigh. Take off cover, skim excess fat from the liquid. Turn heat to medium and baste duck frequently for 15 minutes until the skin is dark brown, and about ½ to 1 cup liquid remains. Serve hot.

This dish has been widely used in restaurant banquets and is also a big dish at home. All participants of my classes enjoy it very much. Even my Chinese friends cook this dish quite often after they have my recipe. In China, as we do not have cook books, we improve our knowledge and technique by experience.

Beef

BEEF IS NOT POPULAR IN CHINA. FIRST, THE BEEF is not very good and only available in big cities. Second, many Chinese who are of the Buddhist faith never eat beef in their whole life. They think that a good bull, cow, or buffalo has worked hard in the fields, therefore it is very cruel to eat their meat. Buddhists believe that cruel persons will be punished by Heaven. Pigs are raised for meat therefore it is not as bad to eat them.

The situation is different here. There is plenty of good beef and it has been raised for the purpose of being eaten and not for work.

Flank steak is most suitable for use in quick-stirring dishes, as the grains or muscles are in same direction which makes cutting easy. Flank steak is tender if cut across the grain in slices or shreds, and the price is comparatively low. If sirloin or top rump is used you may cut the meat into thicker slices or chunks to bring out the full value of this good steak. Because it is beef you can cook it medium rare instead of well done. Flank steak is not so good in chunks.

Pot roast and shank beef are suitable for Spiced Beef with Soy Sauce or any stewing dishes. Do not use good tender steak for these dishes as it is not only a waste of value but also it tastes dry.

Slightly frozen meat is easier to cut. I think it is wise to buy

115

extra flank steaks since they are not always available in the market. Trim them and cut them lengthwise into strips (with the grain) and store them in the freezer for future use. When it is time to use, slightly defrost the strips at room temperature and cut across the grain (crosswise) into small pieces.

Stock made from beef bones is not suitable for Chinese soup, as the odor is very strong.

Lamb and mutton are main meat for Moslems. In Northern China many Chinese are of Moslem faith and are forbidden to eat pork. Since beef is not popular, lamb and mutton are widely used in their dishes. Moslems have clean habits and are good cooks; their dishes are welcomed by a great many Chinese. (Many of them open restaurants.) Lamb Chafing Dish is one of the most famous of these.

1 lb	**beef steak** — sliced. Flank steak is fairly inexpensive and easy to slice.
3 TBS	**soy sauce**
1 TBS	**corn starch**
1 TBS	**dry sherry**
1 tsp	**sugar**
¼ tsp	**M.S.G.**
1 slice	**ginger root**
4 TBS	**cooking oil**
½ tsp	**salt**
¼ lb	**pea pods**

BEEF WITH
PEA PODS
(SNOW PEAS)

SERVINGS:
CHINESE 4-6
AMERICAN 2-3

雪
豆
牛
肉

1. Cut the beef across the grain into thin ¼″ slices about 2″ long.

2. Mix sliced beef with soy sauce, corn starch, sherry, sugar, and M.S.G. Set aside.

3. Remove stems and strings from pea pods. Rinse the pea pods and pat dry with a towel.

Put 2 TBS oil in hot skillet over a high flame. Add salt first and then pea pods, stirring constantly until the pods turn darker green (less than 1 minute). Remove pods and spread out on a plate. In the same skillet, add the remaining 2 TBS oil and ginger root. Stir in beef mixture and turn constantly until the beef is almost cooked (not over 2 minutes). Add pea pods and mix thoroughly. For crispness do not overcook. Serve immediately.

This is a wonderful dish to be served at the family table as well as at a party. Although the pea pods are obtainable only at Chinese groceries, it is worth the trouble to buy them fresh. If you have a vegetable garden you can grow them yourself.

When pea pods are inadequate or unobtainable, substitute sliced bamboo shoots or mushrooms (black or fresh), or sliced tender celery.

BEEF WITH
GREEN
PEPPERS

1 lb	beef steak — sliced
3 TBS	soy sauce
1 TBS	corn starch
1 TBS	dry sherry
1 tsp	sugar
¼ tsp	M.S.G.
1 slice	ginger root
4 TBS	cooking oil
½ tsp	salt
2	green peppers, medium — or 3 small ones (large ones have thicker skin

青
椒
牛
肉

1. Flank steak is fairly inexpensive and easy to slice. Cut the beef across the grain into thin ¼-inch slices about 2 inches long.

2. Mix sliced beef with soy sauce, corn starch, sherry, sugar, and M.S.G. Set aside.

3. Rinse green pepper, then cut in chunks and discard seeds and trim off white soft parts of inside of pepper. (Rinse before cutting so the water will not stay inside the pepper.)

Put 2 TBS oil in hot skillet over a high heat. Add salt first and then green peppers, stirring constantly until the peppers turn darker green (less than 1 minute). Remove green peppers and spread out on a plate. In the same skillet, add the remaining 2 TBS oil and ginger root. Stir in beef mixture and turn constantly until the beef is almost cooked (not over 2 minutes). Add green peppers and mix thoroughly. For crispness do not over-cook. Serve immediately.

118

1 lb	**beef steak** sliced. Flank steak is the best
3 TBS	**soy sauce**
1 TBS	**corn starch**
1 TBS	**dry sherry**
1 tsp	**sugar**
¼ tsp	**M.S.G.**
1 slice	**ginger root** or ¼ cup sliced onion
5 TBS	**cooking oil**
½ tsp	**salt**
½ bunch	**fresh broccoli**

BEEF WITH BROCCOLI

SERVINGS:
CHINESE 4-6
AMERICAN 2-3

甘
藍
牛
肉

1. Cut the beef across the grain in thin ¼″ thick slices about 2″ long.

2. Mix sliced beef with soy sauce, corn starch, sherry, sugar, M.S.G., and set aside.

3. Cut the broccoli into flowerets about 2″ long, peel the stalk and slice into 2″ lengths, less than ½″ thick.

Pour 2 TBS oil in a hot skillet over high heat. Add salt and broccoli. Stir and turn constantly until broccoli is dark green — not over 2 minutes. Remove from skillet and spread out on a plate.

Put remaining 3 TBS oil in same skillet, still over high heat. Add ginger or onion slices. Stir in beef mixture and keep turning constantly until almost done — less than 2 minutes. Add cooked broccoli to the beef and mix thoroughly. Serve immediately.

Cauliflower can be used as a substitute, but cook it 2 minutes longer, until it turns a translucent color on the edges. You may use parboiled broccoli, but it will not be as crunchy and crisp. Broccoli tends to make the oil spatter more than other vegetables and should therefore be thoroughly drained before added to hot oil. The first time you cook this dish, wear rubber gloves and a long sleeve blouse (your husband's old shirt will be good, especially for stirring).

**BEEF WITH
GREEN
BEANS**
(String beans)

SERVINGS:
CHINESE 4-6
AMERICAN 2-3

扁
豆
牛
肉

½ lb	**flank steak** sliced into ¼-inch thickness and 2-inch long slices. Sliced pork can be a substitute.
2 TBS	**soy sauce**
1 tsp	**dry sherry**
½ TBS	**corn starch**
1 tsp	**sugar**
1 lb	**green beans** (frozen or parboiled green beans may be used). Wax beans may be substituted.
4 TBS	**cooking oil**
1 tsp	**salt**
¼ tsp	**M.S.G.**

1. Mix sliced steak with soy sauce, sherry, corn starch and sugar in a bowl and set aside.

2. Remove stems and strings from beans, break or cut into 2 or 3 sections. Wash and drain very well.

Put 2 TBS oil in hot skillet over a high heat. Add in the beef mixture, stirring constantly for 1 minute. Remove the beef into the mixing bowl. (If pork is used, then increase the cooking period to 2 or 3 minutes.)

Add remaining 2 TBS oil in the same skillet. (Do not worry about the gravy which is left in the skillet.) Stir beans into the skillet, then add ½ cup water and bring to a boil. Cook over medium low heat with cover on for 10 minutes, stirring occasionally. If the liquid is about to cook away, then add another ¼ cup of water. If you prefer the beans cooked tender and soft, then cook 5-10 minutes longer and add more water.

Add salt, M.S.G. and the cooked beef into the skillet with the beans. Mix well and serve hot.

120

1 lb	**beef steak** — sliced	
3 TBS	**soy sauce**	
1 TBS	**corn starch**	
1 TBS	**dry sherry**	
1 tsp	**sugar**	
¼ tsp	**M.S.G.**	
1 slice	**ginger root** — or ¼ cup sliced onion	
4 TBS	**cooking oil**	
½ tsp	**salt**	
6-8 oz	**fresh mushrooms** (about 3 or 4 cups) or two 4-oz canned French mushrooms	

BEEF WITH MUSHROOMS

SERVINGS:
CHINESE 4-6
AMERICAN 2-3

香菇牛肉

Cut beef across the grain in thin ¼-inch thick slices about 2 inches long. Mix sliced beef with soy sauce, corn starch, sherry, sugar, M.S.G., and set aside. Cut the fresh mushrooms into slices ¼-inch thick.

Pour 2 TBS oil in a hot skillet over high heat. Add salt and mushrooms. Stir and turn constantly until mushrooms are wilted, about 2 minutes. Remove from skillet and spread out on a plate.

Put remaining 2 TBS oil in same skillet, still over high heat. Add ginger or onion slices. Stir in beef mixture and keep turning constantly until almost done — less than 2 minutes. Add cooked mushrooms to the beef and mix thoroughly. Serve immediately.

This is a westernized Chinese dish. Most restaurants use canned French mushrooms because it is neat and lighter in color. But fresh mushrooms are more delicious, so you can use either according to your choice and convenience. If you are fond of Chinese mushrooms, even they can be used. (Soften them before cooking.)

121

CHUNGKING BEEF SHREDS — HOT

SERVINGS:
CHINESE 4-6
AMERICAN 2-3

乾
炒
牛
肉
絲

1 lb	**beef steak** — shredded very fine (Flank steak is best. For easy cutting, freeze the beef slightly.)
3 TBS	**soy sauce**
1 tsp	**dry sherry**
¾ cup	**cooking oil**
1 TBS	**ginger root** — peeled and shredded very fine
1 TBS	**hot pepper flakes**
½ cup	**carrot** — peeled and shredded very fine
1 cup	**stringed celery stalks** — very fine shreds. Do not use leaves.
1 tsp	**salt**
¼ tsp	**M.S.G.**

Mix beef, soy sauce, and sherry. Set aside.

Pour ½ cup of oil into a hot skillet. Add beef mixture and stir constantly over high flame for 8 to 10 minutes or more until the edges of the beef are browned. Remove beef and oil to a colander or strainer over a large bowl. Save the liquid for gravy over the rice.

Add remaining ¼ cup oil to the same skillet. Cook the ginger root first, then hot pepper flakes and carrot. Stir for ½ minute and add celery for another ½ minute, stirring constantly. Add the cooked and drained beef, salt, and M.S.G. and remove from the heat. Serve immediately.

This is a famous Chungking dish. It is the only one which does not call for corn starch mixed with the small pieces of meat, as the beef in this dish should be dry and chewy. The carrot and celery should be crisp. Use more or less of hot pepper flakes according to your taste. You may substitute fresh hot pepper shreds (½ to 1 cup).

The family stove does not give heat as high as at a restaurant, and the beef may not be so dry, but it is delicious anyway, especially for the person who loves hot dishes.

This recipe is added at the request of our friend and fellow-gourmet, Mr. H. Vose Greenough, Jr.

122

3-4 lb	**beef pot roast** — or boneless chuck	
1 TBS	**dry sherry**	
⅓ cup	**soy sauce**	
2 slices	**ginger root**	
½ TBS	**star anise cloves**	
2 TBS	**sugar**	

SPICED BEEF WITH SOY SAUCE

SERVINGS:
CHINESE 10
AMERICAN 5-8

五香牛肉

Put all the ingredients in a heavy pot with 1 cup of water. Bring to a boil. Simmer with cover over very low heat for 3 hours or more until tender. Turn occasionally for even flavor and prevent sticking to bottom of pot and burning. If the cover is not tight enough or the heat is too high, then the liquid dries out before the beef is tender. Add a little water, ¼-½ cup, as needed.

You may serve it either cold or hot in slices.

In China it is a dish especially good for picnics.

If you want to speed the simmer period, then cut the beef in chunks. It takes about half the time to be tender, then increase soy sauce to ½ cup.

JELLIED LAMB LOAF

SERVINGS:
CHINESE 8-10
AMERICAN 6

2-3 lb	**lamb fores, shoulder chops, or stew cuts** (The leg and chops have more meat and fewer bones but cost more.)
½ cup	**soy sauce**
2 TBS	**sugar**
1 TBS	**dry sherry**
1	**carrot** — cut into 3 or 4 sections
2½ cups	**water or stock**

Put all the above ingredients in a saucepan or Dutch oven. Bring to a boil, cover, and simmer for 1½ to 2 hours until the meat is very tender. Stir occasionally to prevent burning. Remove the pan from the heat and let cool.

Drain off the liquid which should be about 2 cups. If there is not enough, add water to make 2 cups and return the liquid to the pan. Skim off the fat.

Pick off the meat from the bones and discard the carrot, bones and big pieces of fat. Return the boned meat to the pan containing the liquid and bring to a boil. Remove from heat and add the following ingredients:

2 TBS	**plain gelatine** — softened in a cup of cold water.
¼ tsp	**M.S.G.**
½ tsp	**salt** (or to taste, as the saltiness of soy sauce varies.)
scallion or parsley garnish	

Pour the whole thing into a loaf pan to cool, then store in refrigerator to set firm. Serve cold in slices or squares. Or take the whole loaf out by dipping the loaf pan in hot water for a second or two and turning it

124

upside down on an oblong or oval plate. Garnish with minced or shredded scallion or parsley, and decorate as you desire.

This is a good, economical and easy dish. It is wonderful to serve at parties as an appetizer or side dish and can be kept nicely in the refrigerator for a few days.

In ancient China, "jellied lamb with fine wine 羊羔美酒 " was among the most enjoyable things for poets, philosophers and scholars. Even now it is still the favorite dish of many people. My father was fond of it. Lamb is supposed to be "warm" so it is widely relished in winter. The refrigerator, however, has not yet become common in China, so we make jellied lamb only in the winter to have it set firm. We used pig rind for the jelly, added during the cooking. Here, the plain gelatine is more convenient.

Pork

PORK IS THE MAJOR MEAT IN CHINA. WHEN WE say meat we usually mean pork. Pork is more tender than beef and does not have a strong odor. Almost any part of the lean meat is tender in pork, but for the work and money involved the following information is useful.

For Chinese cooking the Boston butt is the best buy. (It gets its name from the city where first it was cut this way.) One piece can be used in several different dishes and with the convenience of the refrigerator and freezer, you can save the extra meat for future use. You will enjoy the savings also. Boston butt is normally about 3½ to 4½ lbs. and is located above and next to the picnic shoulder. It has only one triangle-shaped bone and no skin. A big piece of lean meat, about 1 lb., the so-called *eye,* in the center next to the bone is tender and juicy and the best of the pork meat. It is suitable for quick-stirring dishes, in soup, or Pork Strips. The meat along the bone, very lean but with gristle, should be trimmed and may be cut in small pieces or ground up. The rest of the meat is mixed with fat, the larger pieces of which should be trimmed off and discarded. When ground, this part of the meat is wonderful to use in Wonton filling, meat balls, and Lion's Head (page 136). Simmer the bone with 4½ cups of water and 1 tsp dry sherry for ½ hour or more for soup stock.

Picnic shoulder has too large a bone, too much gristle and

126

skin. It is not suitable for quick-stirring dishes requiring lean meat. It can be cooked only for long-simmering dishes such as Shanghai Ham.

Fresh ham is a very large piece of pork, about 12 to 16 lbs., and is usually too big for regular family use. Generally half a ham is available in the market. The shank end of a half ham is good for Shanghai Ham, but can still be bigger than needed. Ask the butcher to cut off a piece of center ham slice, which is excellent for use in quick-stirring dishes. Fresh ham is too lean for grinding.

Pork tenderloin and Canadian fresh bacon are most suitable for Pork Strips (page 72).

Pork tenderloin cutlet and pork chops are good for Pork Chops Chinese Style (page 131). For soup, you can use a small amount of lean meat cut from a chop.

Pork feet and hocks may be cooked the same way as Shanghai Ham, but pork feet are better to serve cold than hot.

Many Chinese are fond of pork fat and skin, which are cooked very tender. Fresh belly bacon (with skin) is very popular for such dishes, but since it is too fat I do not recommend it.

For Barbecued Spare Ribs do not use the cut called "country style" unless you separate the meat from the bones.

Pork stomach and kidney are among the delicacies in China and are often served at banquets.

PORK WITH	1 cup	**lean pork** — shredded (about ½ lb)
BEAN	2 TBS	**soy sauce**
SPROUTS	1 tsp	**dry sherry**

PORK WITH
BEAN
SPROUTS

SERVINGS:
CHINESE 4-5
AMERICAN 2-3

1 cup	**lean pork** — shredded (about ½ lb)
2 TBS	**soy sauce**
1 tsp	**dry sherry**
¼ tsp	**M.S.G.**
1½ TBS	**corn starch**
1 tsp	**salt**
1 stalk	**scallion** — cut into shreds
4 cups	**bean sprouts** — packed tightly (about 1 lb)
3 TBS	**cooking oil**

豆
芽
肉
絲

1. Mix pork shreds with soy sauce, sherry, M.S.G. and ½ TBS corn starch in a bowl and set aside.

2. Mix 1 TBS corn starch with 3 TBS cold water in a small bowl.

Pour the oil into a hot skillet over medium heat. Add salt and scallion, stir for a few seconds, then add the mixed pork. Stir constantly, about 3 to 4 minutes, until the pork is cooked. Stir in the bean sprouts for 1 minute till they are half translucent. Add the well-stirred corn starch mixture. Stir well until the liquid is thickened (less than 1 minute). Serve hot.

You will enjoy the sweetness of fresh bean sprouts in this dish. Do not use canned bean sprouts. (See page 52 for How to Grow Bean Sprouts at Home.) Re-heated bean sprouts shrink and lose their good texture.

½ cup	**lean pork** — shredded (about ¼ lb)	
¼ cup	**dried Chinese wood ears** (black fungus)	
½ cup	**dried golden needles** (tiger lily)	
4	**eggs** — beaten	
1 tsp	**dry sherry**	
2 TBS	**soy sauce**	
1 tsp	**corn starch**	
¼ tsp	**M.S.G.**	
3 TBS	**oil**	
1 slice	**ginger root**	
1 stalk	**scallion** — shredded	
1 tsp	**salt**	

MANDARIN MOO SHI PORK

SERVINGS:
CHINESE 4-6
AMERICAN 2-3

木犀肉

1. Pour boiling water over wood ears, cover and soak for 15 minutes until soft. Clean, rinse and drain. Same for golden needles.

2. Mix pork with sherry, soy sauce, M.S.G. and corn starch.

Heat 2 TBS oil in skillet over medium heat. Add ginger slice. Scramble eggs into fine pieces and remove from skillet. Stir and cook the mixed pork in the same skillet with remaining 1 TBS oil. Add scallion, then wood ears, tiger lily and salt, stirring constantly about 3 minutes. Return scrambled eggs to skillet, mix well and serve hot with Mandarin thin pancakes. See page 203.

Do not add any water, this dish should be dry.

This is one of the most popular dishes served with Mandarin pancakes. When served at restaurants, it is enriched by adding mushrooms, bamboo shoots, cabbage, etc. I think at home it causes more work to prepare so many ingredients. Besides, why not keep it the authentic way!

Most people, even Chinese, when they have this dish always ask me how the pan-

129

cakes are made so thin. Now they will be delighted to know how to make them. See page 203 for recipe. It will come out satisfactorily as I have tried it on many people, even teenagers. Just read recipe and study illustrations carefully.

PORK WITH BEAN THREAD (CHINESE VERMICELLI)

SERVINGS:
CHINESE 4-6
AMERICAN 2-3

1 cup	**lean pork** — shredded (about ½ lb)
1 tsp	**dry sherry**
1 tsp	**corn starch**
¼ tsp	**M.S.G.**
2 TBS	**soy sauce**
¼ lb	**bean thread** — dried
½ cup	**leek or scallion** — finely shredded
3 TBS	**cooking oil**
1 tsp	**salt**

1. Mix pork, sherry, corn starch, M.S.G. and soy sauce in a bowl and set aside.

2. Soak bean thread in hot water until soft, about 5-10 minutes, then break them in short lengths, about 8 inches, by hand, knife or scissors. Drain well.

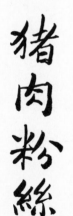

Heat skillet, add oil, salt, and leek shreds, stirring constantly over medium high heat until leeks become wilted, about ½ minute. Put in pork mixture and stir for about 3-4 minutes or until no more blood comes out and the pork is well cooked. Add ¼ cup water and bean thread and continue stirring over medium heat for 2 minutes until the bean thread turns transparent. If the bean thread becomes too sticky to stir, then add 2 TBS or more of water. Serve immediately.

Bean thread has more texture than flavor; actually it has no flavor in itself but

130

absorbs the flavor from the gravy or soup. Therefore, be careful not to overcook it. Just stir it constantly until it is hot and absorbs the gravy evenly. Always serve bean thread *immediately* after cooking; otherwise it turns gluey and loses its smooth texture.

Shredded Chinese celery cabbage, bamboo shoots, and/or mushrooms may be added. Even crab meat can be substituted for pork.

---

4 pcs	**pork chops** or pork tenderloin	
½ cup	**onion** — sliced shreds	
3 TBS	**soy sauce**	
1 TBS	**sugar** — golden brown is better	
¼ tsp	**M.S.G.**	
1 TBS	**cooking oil**	

PORK CHOP SHANGHAI STYLE

SERVINGS:
CHINESE 4
AMERICAN 2-3

红
燒
排
骨

Mix the soy sauce, sugar, and M.S.G. with ½ cup water in a small bowl.

Put the oil in a hot skillet over medium high heat. Spread the pork chops on the bottom of skillet. Brown both sides. Then remove chops to a plate and leave as much oil as possible in the skillet. Stir in the onion until edges are light brown. Return the chops to skillet with the onion. Pour the soy sauce mixture over chops and cover. Cook slowly for 5 minutes and turn once for even color and flavor. Remove cover and baste for ½ minute and serve hot.

This is almost the only way to cook pork chops in China. Cook with or without onion as you desire. Never cover them before serving as the dripping of steam may discolor the nice brown appearance. (This is the same for all food cooked with a large amount of soy sauce.)

131

CHUNGKING PORK

SERVINGS:
CHINESE 4-6
AMERICAN 2-3

1 lb	lean pork
1 tsp	dry sherry
3 slices	ginger root
4 TBS	cooking oil
¼ lb	regular cabbage — cut in pieces 2" x 2" — about 2 or 3 cups
½ tsp	salt
2 cloves	garlic — crushed
¼ cup	black beans — minced
1 tsp	hot pepper flakes or powder
2 TBS	soy sauce
¼ cup	stock from cooking pork
¼ tsp	M.S.G.

回
鍋
肉

1. Simmer the pork in a small sauce pan with 2 cups of water, sherry and 1 slice ginger for ½ hour until tender. Remove the sauce pan from heat and let cool.

2. Cut the cooked pork into large slices about ¼-inch thick and reserve the stock for later use.

Put 2 TBS oil in a hot skillet over medium heat. Add salt, then cabbage, stirring constantly for one minute. When the cabbage is half translucent, remove and spread on a plate.

Pour the remaining 2 TBS oil in the same skillet over medium heat. Add the remaining 2 slices ginger, crushed garlic and minced black beans for a few stirrings, then add hot pepper flakes and sliced pork. Pour in the soy sauce, stock and M.S.G. Stir and cook for 1 minute. Mix in the cooked cabbage and serve immediately.

This is one of the best known Szechuan dishes. It has been enjoyed very much by many Americans who like spiced food. Translated literally, it is "Return to pan Meat" which means the meat in this dish has been cooked twice. In China, when we say meat we mean pork. Otherwise it will be called beef meat or lamb meat.

If you prefer a very hot dish, then increase the hot pepper flakes to your taste (finer pepper flakes or powder is better).

Many people like to add Hoi Sin sauce instead of black beans to this dish. You may do the same, but it is not authentic. Only soy bean paste can be used and still be authentic.

---

1 cup	**pork** — shredded (about ½ lb lean pork)	
1 pkg	**frozen green peas**— 10 oz. (about 1 lb fresh peas with shell)	
1 tsp	**dry sherry**	
2 tsp	**corn starch**	
¼ tsp	**M.S.G.**	
1 TBS	**soy sauce**	
2 TBS	**cooking oil**	
1 tsp	**salt**	
1 slice	**ginger**	

PORK WITH GREEN PEAS

SERVINGS:
CHINESE 4-6
AMERICAN 2-3

1. Mix the shredded pork with sherry, 1 tsp corn starch, M.S.G. and soy sauce in a bowl and set aside.

2. Defrost the frozen peas by soaking in hot water, and then drain. If fresh peas are used, then shell the peas and parboil them for 2 minutes. Rinse in cold water and drain.

3. Mix 1 tsp corn starch with 2 TBS water.

Put oil in a hot deep skillet or sauce pan over medium heat. Add the ginger, salt and the pork mixture. Stir constantly for 3 to 4 minutes until the pork changes color and is cooked. Add the peas and stir for another 2 minutes. Stir in the corn starch mixture until liquid thickens. Serve hot.

133

MANDARIN SWEET AND SOUR PORK

SERVINGS:
CHINESE 4-6
AMERICAN 2-3

甜
酸
肉

Meat —

2 cups	**cubed lean pork** (about 1 lb) free from gristle and fat
1 TBS	**dry sherry**
1 TBS	**soy sauce**
3 TBS	**corn starch**
½ tsp	**salt**
2 cups	**cooking oil**

Mix thoroughly all above ingredients (except oil) in a large bowl.

Separate pieces and fry in the oil (350°) until well done and crisp on edges (about 8 minutes). Drain oil from fried pork and spread out on absorbent paper. Keep in warm place or low oven.

Sweet and Sour Sauce —

⅔ cup	**sugar**
¼ cup	**catsup**
⅓ cup	**water or pineapple juice**
½ cup	**cider vinegar**
2 TBS	**soy sauce**

Mix well together above ingredients and set aside.

1 clove	**crushed garlic**
1 TBS	**cooking oil**
2 TBS	**corn starch** (mix with ⅓ cup water)
1 cup	**pineapple chunks** — drained well

Heat sauce pan with oil. Brown garlic and then discard. Add sugar and vinegar mixture until the mixture starts boiling. Stir in corn starch mixture, stirring constantly until it thickens and becomes translucent. Add pineapple chunks first, then the fried pork. Mix well. Serve immediately.

4 lb	**fresh pork ham,** butt, or shoulder	
1 cup	**soy sauce**	
½ cup	**sugar** — or less	
1 TBS	**dry sherry**	
2 slices	**ginger root** — or 2 cloves garlic	
few cloves	**star anise**	
½-1 cup	**water**	

Sear and scald the pork by soaking it in boiling water for a few minutes. Rinse with cold water (See page 31).

Place the pork with all the ingredients in a large sauce pan, Dutch oven, or pressure cooker, without using pressure cap. Bring to a boil, cover and simmer. (If using pressure cooker, reduce water to ½ cup.) Turn the pork over occasionally until tender — about 2 hours or more. Remove cover and increase heat. Baste the pork until about 1 cup liquid remains (about 15 or 20 minutes). Skim fat and serve it hot or cold.

Like Shanghai Duck, this is very popular in China. Butt and shoulder can be used in the same way but ham has more lean meat. We cook pig's feet in this way to serve with drinks at home or with close friends, but not at formal parties, as the way of eating is not very graceful. You cannot enjoy pig's feet unless you can hold them with your fingers.

The left-over gravy and pieces of meat are wonderful to cook with soy sauce eggs. (See page 161.)

135

LION'S HEAD

4 cups	**pork** — ground (2 lb-⅔ lean and ⅓ fat)
⅓ cup	**soy sauce**
½ cup	**water** — cold
½ TBS	**dry sherry**
1 tsp	**golden brown sugar**
1 tsp	**salt**
½ tsp	**M.S.G.**
4 TBS	**corn starch**
2 TBS	**cooking oil**
2 lb	**Chinese cabbage** or Chinese celery cabbage — about 1 large head. Regular cabbage is not suitable as it has a strong odor.

獅
子
頭

1. Trim gristle off meat. Grind meat through the blades with medium holes. Run half the meat through a second time.

2. Combine all meat, soy sauce, water, sherry, sugar, salt, M.S.G. and 1 TBS corn starch in a large bowl and let set for 15 minutes. Divide into 6 or 8 portions.

3. Mix in a deeper plate the remaining 3 TBS corn starch with 2 TBS cold water into a thin paste.

4. Wash the cabbage and cut leaves and stems into 2-inch sections and set aside.

Pour oil in skillet over medium heat. Form one portion of the mixed pork into large ball and use hands to coat the meatball with the corn starch paste. Toss the meatball between the hands for even coating. It is quite sticky with rough surface which will be smoothed after cooking. (Rinsing your hands in cold water will make the surface of the ball smooth but the water will make oil spatter.)

136

Brown the coated meatballs in the skillet. Always loosen the bottom first with the back of spatula, then turn carefully. Transfer the browned balls very gently to an enameled pot or Dutch oven.

(Keep the skillet and the left-over oil and gravy for later use.)

Add:

½ cup	water
1 tsp	sugar
1½ TBS	soy sauce

to the pot and bring to a boil. Cover and simmer over very low heat for 1½ to 2 hours.

Stir and cook the washed cabbage in the used skillet over medium high heat for 5 minutes. (Add the cabbage little by little as you can fit it into the skillet.) Arrange the cooked cabbage in an oven-proof casserole or enamel-coated pot. Set the meatballs (with gravy) on top of the cabbage and simmer for 10 minutes; or place the pot in medium oven for 15 to 20 minutes. Skim fat from gravy. Serve hot from the casserole or enameled pot.

New customers of our restaurant are always surprised about this dish and ask if it is really made from lion's head. Of course it is not.

Chinese people like to put words like dragon, phoenix, or lion into names of dishes, because in Imperial China, dragon and phoenix symbolized emperors and their empresses. So, to use these names indicates the high quality of the food. As for lion, it is king of the jungle. To use its name means high quality and large size. In the menu, Lion's Head is actually large meatballs, the size of a baseball or tennis ball.

This is a most famous dish from Yang Chow, which is close to Nanking. The best preparation of the meat should be to cut finely and chop coarsely. I found grinding the meat through the medium holes will get the same result, but the gristle must be removed entirely before grinding.

137

Good Lion's Head should be very tender and cannot be picked up by chopsticks. You have to use a spoon.

In China we use half lean and half fat to make the meatballs tender and juicy. I reduce the fat to 1/3 and up the lean to 2/3 for health reasons. After cooking, most fat is floating on top of the gravy and should be skimmed off before serving.

Left-over Lion's Head can be reheated nicely without losing flavor.

Crabmeat (about 1 cup or one 6½ oz. can, flaked and soft bone removed) may be added to the pork mixture; then you should reduce the soy sauce to 2 tbs and increase the salt to 2 tsp.

The old way is to put the cabbage in the bottom of pot and simmer with the meatballs for a long period. I think the cabbage is too much over-cooked this way and loses the texture and food value. It is also messy looking.

You may cook the balls a day ahead and cook the cabbage with the meatballs just before you are ready to serve. It may also be kept warm in low oven until time to serve.

STUFFED CUCUMBERS

SERVINGS:
CHINESE 4-6
AMERICAN 2-3

2	**cucumbers**— each about 8 to 10 inches long.
1 cup	**ground pork** — about ½ lb.
½ cup	**corn flakes or bread crumbs**
1 tsp	**dry sherry**
2 TBS	**soy sauce**
2 TBS	**corn starch**
¼ tsp	**M.S.G.**
2 TBS	**cooking oil**
½ tsp	**salt**
½ tsp	**sugar**

1. Peel cucumbers and cut off both ends (more on the stem end), then cut crosswise into about 2-inch sections. Hollow out inside, discarding the seedy portion.

2. Mix meat with corn flakes, sherry 1½ TBS soy

138

sauce, 1 TBS corn starch, M.S.G., and 3 TBS water. Set aside.

3. Fill the cavities of the cucumber sections tightly with the meat mixture, rounding it out at the ends to allow for shrinkage and to prevent the stuffing from slipping out of the cucumbers. Dip ends in flour for less sticking.

4. Mix 1 TBS corn starch with ¼ cup water.

Place oil in hot skillet over medium heat and put in cucumber sections on end to brown well. Turn and brown other end. Then lay the cucumbers on their sides, add 1 cup water, ½ TBS soy sauce, salt, and sugar. Cover and boil on low heat about 20 minutes until cucumbers are translucent and tender. (Turn occasionally for even cooking). Remove cover and baste for 5 minutes. Thicken the gravy with the corn starch mixture and serve hot. This dish can be covered and kept warm in a low oven until ready to serve.

This is a typical family dish, not available in restaurants. It is easy to cook and keep warm until the time to serve. You may use hamburg instead of pork. If you have any stuffing left over, form it into balls and cook them along with the cucumbers.

STEAMED MEAT CAKE

SERVINGS:
CHINESE 4-6
AMERICAN 2-3

蒸
肉
餅

1½ cups	**ground pork** — good hamburger may be used
¼ cup	**water chestnuts** — minced
¼ cup	**black mushrooms** — softened and minced
⅓ cup	**Smithfield ham** — minced
1 TBS	**soy sauce**
1 tsp	**dry sherry**
½ tsp	**salt**
¼ tsp	**golden brown sugar**
1 TBS	**corn starch**
¼ tsp	**M.S.G.**
½ TBS	**ginger root** — minced or shredded
½ TBS	**scallion** — minced or shredded

Mix all the ingredients in a mixing bowl thoroughly or by the hands.

Press the mixed meat into a flat cake evenly in a deep plate or shallow bowl (heat proof).

Set the steamer (into which the plate will fit) with 4 cups of water or more to boil.

Place the plate into steamer (page 34) over medium heat. Steam for 10 to 15 minutes (depending on the thickness of the meat cake), until the meat is cooked and has liquid around the cake. Since it is pork you must make sure it is cooked well. By using a fork open a hole in the center of cake to see if meat is raw or not. If raw, steam for another few minutes. Serve hot on the cooking plate at the table. This is an easy dish if the large steamer is available.

Seafood

ONLY A FEW PLACES ALONG THE COAST IN CHINA **LOBSTER**
have lobster. With the poor transportation system,
most Chinese have never seen a lobster in their
whole life, so lobster is not as popular as here.
Fresh water crabs are very common in China.
Americans like live lobsters. Chinese are crazy about live fresh
water crabs. There is a vast difference between the texture and
flavor of a lobster or crab when it is cooked live or dead. The
same is true of other seafood. If the lobster is cooked alive its
meat will be smooth and have a little spring when chewed on
(this texture is described as *live* by Chinese) and will be shiny.
The meat is also easier to remove from the shell; so use only live
lobsters in Lobster with Meat Sauce, page 151.

The late fall, when the first west and north winds arrive, is
the best season for crabs; also the chrysanthemums are in bloom
in China. It is a treat between family and close friends, eating
steamed live fresh water crabs and at the same time enjoying the
beauty and fragrance of chrysanthemums. After eating we wash
our hands with chrysanthemum leaves as you would use lemon.
Ginger tea is also served.

Since it is impossible to get fresh water crabs here, we have **CRAB**
enjoyed live salt-water crabs. I cook them in the same manner as

141

fresh-water crabs in the shell in China. I did not list those recipes in this book as I understand most Americans do not have the patience to eat them, and also it is not easy to get live crabs in the market. If you happen to like crabs or if you can easily get them alive, then use the same recipe as for lobster. We also use crabmeat in many delicate dishes such as wonton filling, soup, and mixed into Lion's Head. I will not expect you to take out the meat from a cooked crab in such a busy American life, so the canned or packaged crabmeat is good to use.

SHRIMP

Shrimp is a very delicate type food in China. We prefer fresh-water shrimps, called prawns, which are sold live at the market in the morning. At banquets the prawn is a must in dishes such as Shrimp with Peas, etc. It is served the first of many fancy dishes. With careful and skillful cooking, these tiny prawns are very tender and succulent. In many resorts, restaurants serve the fresh water prawns and fish almost in a from-water-to-mouth manner. They keep the prawns and the fish alive in a covered basket and soak the basket in the nearby pond, lake, or river. When customers place the order, then they start to cook. Sometimes the kitchen helper brings in the live fish to kill it in front of you, assuring you it is freshly killed. There is a live fresh-water prawn dish which is not cooked. The live prawns are clipped of claws and served in a plate with a bowl covering it. When you eat them just open the bowl a little bit and catch the live prawn with your chopsticks and dip it in a kind of sauce, shelling it while eating it. Maybe you would be scared to eat it, but to many people it is an incomparable delicacy. This is the same as Americans who eat raw steak.

As prawn is tiny in China and shrimp is comparatively large in this country, buy smaller shrimps to cook with for recipes in this book or cut large ones into smaller pieces. We cook prawns

142

with or without shell. Chinese are very capable to shell the prawn in the mouth with chopsticks (it is not bad manners), but it is quite impossible for Americans. I have had to give up those dishes which are cooked with the shell in this book. Shelling shrimps at the table with the fingers does not only lose the flavor but also is too messy.

The Chinese are great eaters and great cooks of fish. We **FISH** have so many ways to cook and serve fish. We prefer fresh-water fish to salt-water fish. Chinese are very fussy about the way to handle a fresh-water fish. We never want to kill fish too early before cooking. In other words, although the fish is dead, the body and the meat is still moving. The fresh fish has a smooth texture and a delicious flavor which the Chinese describe as *live*. The dead fish loses these qualities. No Chinese is willing to buy dead fresh-water fish so they are kept alive in a big wooden basin. (Salt-water fish are dead as soon as they come out of the water.) People bring fish home in baskets and keep them alive in water until cooking time. Sometimes we keep the fish in water for two or three days to get out the muddy odor from fish such as carp. In case the fish seems weak we would rather kill it before it dies naturally. Fresh salt-water fish are only available along the sea-coast provinces. Some salt-water fish are very delicious and have very smooth fine meat. In Chinese cooking the fish should be scaled and cleaned with head and tail intact; discard the gills. In cleaning the cavities you must be very gentle not to break the gall bladder which is a small yellowish blue sac and tastes bitter. (In case it breaks then rub with some kitchen soda and rinse.) The air bladder, roe, and lungs are good to eat, if the fish is very fresh. The lungs and cleaned intestines, etc., of a kind of big fresh-water fish can be cooked into a famous dish. Many Chinese are fond of fish heads, especially the cheek meat and tongue. One

143

kind of large fish head, fins and tail, is a delicacy to the Chinese. We never skin the fish unless we are just using the fish meat. The skin is good to eat, too. Some kinds of fish have no scale such as butterfish, eels, etc. Fish like shad should not be scaled. Because this kind of fish has very fine meat, we want the scales to protect the fish from being over-cooked (generally it is steamed). Under the scales is a thin layer of fat which keeps the meat juicy. I remember a story which my mother told me. In the old days in China after three days of wedding, the bride must go to the kitchen to cook something for the parents-in-law. In this way she can show her skill and pay her respects to the elder generation. This was quite a job to cook in a strange kitchen under all the watching eyes (Chinese keep big families), particularly the so-called sharp-mouthed sister-in-law (husband's sister). This bride in our story decided to cook the steamed shad. First, she scaled the fish. All the people started laughing at her in a mocking way, since shad should not be scaled. But the calm bride used a fine needle to sew the scales together into a blanket, as one would sew on sequins. She put the scale blanket back on the fish to steam. When the parents-in-law ate that fish there was no bother with the scales. Certainly everybody admired her talent, including the sister-in-law. Maybe this is just a story, but you can imagine how the Chinese work to make food taste better and eat easier.

In this country, it is very hard to get live fresh-water fish unless you go fishing for it. If you are lucky to have a fisherman in your family, then you can enjoy the recipe — West Lake Sweet & Sour Fish (page 155). Any meaty fish will be good; I tried large-mouthed bass and had very good results. All kinds of perch, small-mouthed bass, etc., are better for cooking with soy sauce (page 152). Trout, eel, catfish, etc. are fish with very fine smooth meat and are good for steaming. If the fish is too big for the skillet or pan, then cut it into 2 or 3 pieces. Save the fish raw for later cooking.

144

Salt-water sea bass is good for most of the dishes. Flounder and butterfish are better for steamed fish. Scup is better for soy sauce fish. Most of all, the fresh fish is the best to use.

Fish cannot be over-cooked or it will lose its nice texture. For the beginner cook it is better to check by using a small sharp knife, cutting the heavy fish back next to bone to see if the meat is white. If it is still translucent and pink it needs a little more cooking, about 3 to 10 minutes, depending on how thick the area is.

Never reheat left-over fish. Left-over soy sauce fish is good to eat cold. Steamed fish and sweet and sour fish are only good when served hot.

Since Chinese dishes require whole fish and are limited by the size of skillet or steamer, I think the best size of whole fish is about 10″— 12″ long and 1—1½ lb in weight.

If the fish is too small, then use two, such as butter fish. If too big, then cut in half or cut off the head (since not many Americans enjoy the head anyway).

FRIED SHRIMP CHINESE STYLE

SERVINGS:
CHINESE 4-6
AMERICAN 2-3

清炒蝦仁

1 lb	**fresh or frozen raw shrimp**
4-5 drops	**fresh ginger juice** (squeeze minced ginger root in garlic squeezer)
1 tsp	**dry sherry**
1 tsp	**corn starch**
1 tsp	**salt**
¼ tsp	**M.S.G.**
1 stalk	**scallion** — cut into pieces 2 inches long
1 cup	**cooking oil**
2 slices	**fresh ginger root**

Rinse and shell shrimp. Remove intestinal vein (slitting the shrimp down the back and lifting out the black vein). Slice shrimp diagonally into 3 or 4 equal pieces. Mix well with ginger juice, sherry, corn starch, salt, M.S.G. and scallion.

Heat 1 cup oil in skillet over high heat until hot, about 375°. Add slices of ginger root. Stir in shrimp mixture and keep turning constantly, about 1½ minutes until shrimps are pink. Drain in a colander, remove ginger and scallion pieces, serve shrimp immediately.

Actually, the best way of cooking shrimp meat is deep frying rather than quick stirring (saute). Since the delicate meat of shrimp is easily over-cooked or unevenly cooked, the large amount of oil can make the shrimps cook quickly and evenly. Meanwhile, the oil seals in the flavor and moisture.

This is an excellent way to prepare shrimp for any dish calling for cooked shrimp. It is particularly successful in shrimp cocktail or hors d'oeuvres as this method ensures juicy tenderness. Boiling in water tends to make the shrimp dry and tough.

If whole shrimp are preferred, reduce heat and cook slightly longer.

This is the most popular shrimp dish at banquets. Many people like to sprinkle some ground white pepper or dip in vinegar at the table.

Green peas, diced Smithfield ham, water chestnuts and/or bamboo shoots may be added for decoration and more flavor. The main reason for adding these ingredients is because shrimp is expensive and sometimes the live prawn supply is limited at the market. (See next recipe for Shrimp with Peas.)

---

1 lb	**raw shrimp**
4-5 drops	**ginger juice**
1 tsp	**dry sherry**
2 tsp	**corn starch**
1½ tsp	**salt**
½ tsp	**M.S.G.**
1 stalk	**scallion** — cut into 2″ long sections
1 cup	**green peas** — parboiled or frozen (defrost by soaking in hot water and drain)
1 cup	**cooking oil**

SHRIMP WITH GREEN PEAS

SERVINGS:
CHINESE 4-6
AMERICAN 2-3

豌
豆
蝦
仁

1. Prepare the shrimps according to the previous recipe and mix the shrimp with ginger juice, sherry, 1 tsp corn starch, 1 tsp salt, ¼ tsp M.S.G., and scallion in a bowl.

2. Mix the remaining 1 tsp corn starch with 2 TBS cold water in a bowl. Set aside.

Heat oil in skillet over high heat. Stir in mixed shrimp and turn constantly until shrimp turns pink — about 1 minute. Drain the shrimp in colander over a bowl. Discard the scallion. Put 2 TBS oil from the bowl in the same skillet over medium heat. Add the remaining ½ tsp salt and green peas. Stir for 1 minute until the peas are thoroughly heated. Mix in the ¼ tsp M.S.G., then the well-stirred corn starch mixture. When the liquid thickens add the cooked shrimp. Mix well and serve immediately.

Pea pods may be used as a substitute for green peas. Or add diced Smithfield ham, water chestnuts and bamboo shoots to the peas, cutting the portion of peas from 1 cup to ½ cup, making 1½ cups of them in all. If Smithfield ham should be used cut down the amount of salt used in the peas from ½ to ¼ tsp.

SHRIMP	1 lb	**raw shrimp**
WITH	1 tsp	**dry sherry**
BLACK	1 tsp	**corn starch**
BEANS	½ tsp	**salt**
SERVINGS:	¼ tsp	**M.S.G.**
CHINESE 4-6	1 TBS	**scallion** — minced
AMERICAN 2-3	1 TBS	**ginger root** — minced
	¼ cup	**black beans**
	1 cup	**cooking oil**

豆豉蝦仁

1. Rinse and shell shrimp. Split the shrimp in half down the back and lift out the black vein.

2. Mix the shrimp with sherry, corn starch, salt and M.S.G.

3. Mince the black beans and mix with 1 TBS water.

Heat oil in hot skillet over high heat. Stir in mixed shrimps and turn constantly for about 1 minute until shrimps are pink. Drain in a colander or strainer over a bowl.

Put 2 TBS oil from the bowl in the same skillet over medium heat. Add the scallion, ginger root and black beans. After several stirrings, mix in the cooked shrimps and serve immediately.

This is a good tasting shrimp dish but is never served at banquets because the black beans spoil the color of the pretty pink shrimps.

If you are fond of garlic, then add a clove crushed with scallion and ginger root in the cooking.

1 lb	raw shrimp
1 TBS	dry sherry
1 TBS	soy sauce
3 TBS	corn starch
½ tsp	salt
2 cups	cooking oil

Sweet and Sour Sauce

1. Rinse and shell shrimp. Split the shrimp in half down the back and lift out the black vein.

2. Mix thoroughly all above ingredients in a large bowl, except the cooking oil.

Separate pieces and fry in the oil (375°) until well done and crisp on the edges (about 3 minutes). Drain oil from fried shrimp and spread out on absorbent paper. Keep in warm place or low oven.

⅔ cup	sugar
¼ cup	catsup
⅓ cup	water or pineapple juice
½ cup	cider vinegar
2 TBS	soy sauce

Mix well together above ingredients and set aside.

1 clove	crushed garlic
1 TBS	cooking oil
2 TBS	corn starch (mix with ⅓ cup water)
1 cup	pineapple chunks — drained well

Heat sauce pan with oil. Brown garlic and then discard. Add sugar and vinegar mixture until the mixture starts boiling. Stir in corn starch mixture, stirring constantly until it thickens and becomes translucent. Add pineapple chunks first, then the fried shrimp. Mix well. Serve immediately.

149

SHRIMP WITH LOBSTER SAUCE

SERVINGS:
CHINESE 4-6
AMERICAN 2-3

1 lb	**raw shrimp**
½ cup	**ground pork** — about ¼
2 tsp	**dry sherry**
2 TBS	**corn starch**
4 TBS	**cooking oil**
2 slices	**ginger root**
2 cloves	**garlic** — crushed
1½ TBS	**black beans** — minced
½ tsp	**salt**
2 TBS	**soy sauce**
¼ tsp	**M.S.G.**
¼ tsp	**sugar**
1	**egg** beaten

蝦
龍
糊

1. Rinse and shell shrimp. Remove intestinal vein.

2. Mix the shrimp with sherry and ½ TBS corn starch.

3. Mix the remaining 1½ TBS corn starch in ¼ cup cold water.

Put oil in hot skillet over medium high heat. Add mixed shrimps and stir constantly for 2 minutes. Remove shrimps and leave as much oil as you can in the skillet.

Return skillet to the heat. Add ginger root, garlic and black beans. After a few stirrings put in the pork, salt, soy sauce, M.S.G., sugar and 1 cup of water. Bring to a boil. Cover and simmer for 2 minutes. Mix in the well-stirred corn starch mixture and shrimps. Add egg with one or two stirrings, then serve hot.

This is an Americanized Chinese dish. Actually there is no lobster in this dish at all; we just use the same kind of sauce which is used in Lobster with Meat Sauce.

To serve this dish on meatless days, you may use minced bamboo shoots, mushrooms, or water chestnuts instead of meat, or just simply omit the meat.

1	**live lobster** — about 1½ to 2 lbs.	
½ cup	**ground pork** — about ¼ lb	
3 TBS	**cooking oil**	
2 slices	**ginger root**	
2 cloves	**garlic** — crushed	
1½ TBS	**black beans** — minced	
2 tsp	**dry sherry**	
½ tsp	**salt**	
1½ TBS	**soy sauce**	
¼ tsp	**M.S.G.**	
¼ tsp	**sugar**	
1½ TBS	**corn starch**	
1	**beaten egg** — medium	

1. Rinse the live lobster in cold water and dry with paper towel. Cut and chop lobster into 14 pcs. as shown.

2. Break the tomalley into smaller pieces in a small bowl with spoon.

3. Mix the corn starch in ¼ cup cold water.

Pour oil in a hot large skillet or saucepan over medium high heat. Put in ginger root, garlic, black beans, pork and tomalley, and stir for 2 to 3 minutes. Add lobster pieces and sherry for just a few stirrings, then add ¾ cup water, salt, soy sauce, M.S.G., sugar. Cover and bring to a boil. Simmer about 3 to 4 minutes until the lobster shell turns to coral red color and the meat to white and pink. For easy stirring, remove lobster to a plate. Stir in corn starch mixture. When liquid thickens, add egg and return lobster to saucepan and mix well.

Lay lobster on cutting board and split as shown. Then cut into 14 pieces as shown with dotted lines. Discard legs, intestine, sacs in tip of head, spongy gills. Be sure to save the tomalley and the coral. Crush the arm shells for easy eating. When cutting lobster live, he will still be moving; if this bothers you, plunge the lobster in boiling water first.

Chinese restaurants in the United States usually cook lobster this way, and is commonly called Lobster, Chinese Style or Cantonese Style. The "clawless" California spiny lobster and the Norway yellow lobster are good to cook in this way. Live crabs may be cooked this way too. For full enjoyment of this dish as well as to eat in the Chinese manner, suck the lobster pieces first then remove the meat. This meat sauce is well known as Lobster Sauce, and it is good to mix with rice.

In the American serving, allow ½ lobster for each person. To have this dish at its best, you must use *live* lobster and cook it as soon as it is chopped.

SOY SAUCE FISH, SHANGHAI STYLE

SERVINGS:
CHINESE 4-5
AMERICAN 2

紅燒魚

1 medium size 1¼-1½ lb	**whole fish** (sea bass, perch, scup, etc.)
¾ tsp	**salt**
½ cup	**cooking oil**
2 slices	**ginger root**
1 bunch	**scallion** cut in halves
⅓ cup	**sliced bamboo shoots**
⅓ cup	**black mushrooms,** softened and sliced.
1 TBS	**dry sherry**
5 TBS	**soy sauce**
2 TBS	**light brown sugar**
¾ cup	**water**

Scale whole fish thoroughly and clean body cavity, leaving head and tail intact. Rinse in cold water and *dry* inside and out with paper towel. Slash crosswise on each side along the backbone, making three equal diagonal cuts, for more even cooking. Dust both sides with ¼ tsp salt and set aside 10 mins. (If the fish is too big to fit into skillet, then cut fish in half.)

Into very hot skillet put oil and ginger root slices. Gently put in fish and fry over medium high heat for about 3 or 4 minutes on each side. Cover skillet to prevent

152

oil from splashing. Remove from burner and turn carefully. Add scallions, bamboo shoots, mushrooms, and return to the heat. When the fish is golden brown, pour off excess oil and add remaining ingredients to skillet, cover, and bring to a boil. Boil slowly over low heat for 3 minutes. Remove cover, increase heat, and baste fish until a little more than ½ cup liquid remains. Serve hot or cold but never re-heat. If the fish is cut into 2 pieces, then put them on the plate as a whole fish and use the scallions (or bamboo shoots and mushrooms) to cover the division.

This is the commonest way in China to cook fish with soy sauce. In Northern China we like to put a small amount of sugar on it, while in the Shanghai area we use lots of sugar. It is much nicer to keep the whole skin of the fish intact when cooking, but even the Chinese are sometimes unable to do so. The following principles will help to attain that goal:

1. Be sure skillet is very hot before adding oil.

2. When fish is golden brown on bottom side, loosen with back of spatula and then turn gently.

In winter, especially for the New Year holidays, we like to cook this dish in large quantities and serve it cold as a side dish or with drinks. Many people like to eat the scallions cooked with the fish, and the jellied gravy is delicious.

1	**strictly fresh fish** (1 to 1½ lb) — sea bass, flounder, butterfish (2 or 3 pcs.) or perch is suitable.
1 tsp	**dry sherry**
½ tsp	**salt**
2 tsp	**soy sauce**
few slices	**Smithfield ham** with fat on
1 tsp	**scallion** — fine shreds
1 tsp	**ginger root** — fine shreds

清蒸魚

1. Scale whole fish thoroughly and clean body cavity. Discard the gills. Rinse in cold water and drain. Slash crosswise on each side along the backbone in the meaty part, making three or four equal diagonal cuts deep to the backbone but not through, for even cooking. Put the fish in a deep plate which will be fitted into the steamer (page 34). If the fish is too big to fit in the deep plate then cut fish in half.

2. Sprinkle the sherry, salt and soy sauce on the fish and spread the ham slices, ginger root and scallion on also.

Place the plate with the fish in steamer with at least 4-6 cups water. Steam over medium high heat for 10 to 15 minutes (about 10 minutes for 1 lb whole fish). Of course the thickness, heavy or flat, of the fish also makes a difference. Never over-steam. The best way to check is to look at the meat at the cut close to the head (that is the thickest part of the fish) when the fish is steamed for 10 minutes, and if the meat is white and not translucent then it is cooked. Otherwise, steam for 3 to 5 minutes more depending on the size of the uncooked area. If the area is small then you may remove from heat as the steam remaining in the steamer will cook that part by serving time. As soon as the fish is cooked, it should be removed in steamer from heat. The fish may be kept warm in steamer for a few minutes before serving.

After steaming there is more liquid than before in the plate which is delicious and good to mix with rice. Many people prefer dipping steamed fish in vinegar, or vinegar and ginger dipping. (page 57)

To make this dish perfect, the fish must be 100% fresh. Do not over-steam. Do not over-season either.

Black mushrooms (softened) and sliced bamboo shoots can be added with ham slices. Minced black beans (about 1 TBS) may be used to sprinkle on the fish before steaming. Sliced pork (with fat) can replace the ham.

Butter fish is small and flat and takes less time to cook, about 8 to 10 minutes.

WEST LAKE SWEET AND SOUR FISH (Especially for Fishermen)

1	**fresh water big mouthed or small mouthed bass** about 1½ lb. to 2 lb. — just caught and strictly fresh.
1 TBS	**dry sherry**
few slices	**ginger root**
½ cup	**sugar**
⅓ cup	**cider vinegar**
1 TBS	**soy sauce**
¼ tsp	**ginger root juice**
1 clove	**garlic** — peeled and crushed may be added to the sauce.
2 TBS	**corn starch**

SERVINGS:
CHINESE 4-5
AMERICAN 2

湖
溜
魚

155

1. Scale whole fish thoroughly and clean body cavity. Discard the gills. Rinse in cold water and drain. Slash crosswise on each side along the backbone in the meaty part, making three equal diagonal cuts for even cooking.

2. Mix the sugar, vinegar, soy sauce, ginger juice and corn starch or garlic in a small sauce pan.

Boil water in a very large pot or oval roaster with cover and the water must be enough to cover the whole fish.

Put the fish gently into the boiling water and add the sherry and ginger slices. Cover tightly and remove from the heat immediately and soak the fish for 15 to 20 minutes. At the same time cook the sugar and vinegar mixture in the sauce pan over medium heat and stir constantly until it thickens. Discard garlic, if used.

Remove the fish from the water very carefully with a big spatula and a big flat plate. Drain off the water very well and place the fish on a large oval serving dish. Then pour the sauce over the fish and serve immediately.

This is the most famous fish in the beautiful West Lake resort in Hangchow. As I said before when you order this fish at the restaurants along West Lake, the chef's helper will bring the live fish to you and slam it to the floor to kill it in front of you so that you will know it is fresh. As this way of cooking makes the fish meat very tender and smooth, only fresh water fish (which has a very fine texture) can be used.

The fish will be cooked by soaking in the boiling water but never boiled in it.

I add this recipe to this book, first, in respect for my husband's home town, Hangchow; second, to delight our American fishermen and the mother or wife who will enjoy it for easy cooking.

Excellent for people who are on low fat diet.

Eggs

CHICKEN EGGS ARE WIDELY USED IN ALL PARTS of the world, as well as in China, but especially those places where the refrigerator is rare. Meat cannot be kept fresh in warm weather without refrigeration or an icebox, but eggs will stay good for many days. Some dishes will have better results with room temperature eggs. Eggs are inexpensive and are also wonderful cooked by themselves or with other ingredients. They can be cooked fast and simply as Folded Fried Eggs and Egg Drop Soup, or prepared with chicken meat in a delicacy dish like Chicken Velvet, Mandarin Eggs or cooked in dessert as Steamed Egg Cake.

Duck eggs are more tough and strong. Chinese do not like them as well as chicken eggs in cooking. They are commonly used to make preserved eggs such as salted eggs and so-called hundred-year-old eggs.

Salted eggs have been preserved in salted water or salted mud for a month or two. Then when they are cooked, usually hard-boiled, the egg white is very salty and the yolk is oily and tasty. Most people like the yolk, but a few people prefer the white. When salty eggs are served there is always a trading around the table with the whites and yolks.

Hundred-year-old egg is a very romantic and exaggerated English name; actually it is about a hundred days old, preserved

157

in lime and mud. The heat of the lime makes the egg white turn to transparent dark brown and the yolk to greenish black. It looks like a piece of antique — probably this is the reason for the name. The best hundred-year-old eggs are from Peking. They are very large and made of goose eggs or jumbo duck eggs. Hundred-year-old eggs do not need to be cooked; just remove the mud and peel the shell, and serve with soy sauce and sesame seed oil. If it is hard to remove the mud, then shell it with the mud and rinse in cold water. In China preserved eggs are served as a side dish or for breakfast with congee. Here, the hundred-year-old eggs are good to serve as hors d'oeuvres in small pieces pierced with tooth-picks. People will be excited with the romantic name.

Western people dye eggs in different colors for Easter; Chinese dye hard boiled eggs red when a baby is born. We send red eggs to relatives and friends, giving notice of the newborn baby. Odd numbers of eggs, usually nine or eleven, mean it is a boy. Even number, usually eight or ten, mean it is a girl. So everybody is busy counting as soon as the red eggs are received.

6	**large egg yolks**	
6 pcs	**water chestnuts** (minced to about ⅓ cup)	
½ tsp.	**salt**	
1 can	**chicken broth** — about 2 cups or cold chicken broth with 1 tsp salt.	
¼ tsp	**M.S.G.**	
3 TBS	**corn starch**	
½ tsp	**dry sherry**	
2 TBS	**Smithfield ham,** cooked and minced	
5 TBS	**cooking oil**	

溜黄菜

Mix together egg yolks, water chestnuts, salt, chicken broth, M.S.G., corn starch and sherry.

Heat oil in skillet over medium heat. Add the egg mixture into skillet, stirring gently and constantly along the bottom and edge in the same direction until the mixture turns to soft, smooth, moist curds. Garnish with minced ham and serve immediately.

This is a famous Peking dish, with a pretty yellow color and a wonderful creamy consistency. You may substitute paprika for the ham. It is a mistake to use egg white in this dish; only the yolk is needed. You may use the yolks left over from making Chicken Velvet or your American dishes.

CRABMEAT WITH EGGS

蟹粉炒蛋

1 can	crabmeat — 6½ oz
6	eggs
1 tsp	sherry
1 tsp	salt
¼ tsp	M.S.G.
⅛ tsp	white pepper (optional)
1 TBS	scallion — minced
4 TBS	cooking oil

1. Flake crabmeat and remove soft bones, if any, and put the crabmeat with the liquid in a medium mixing bowl.

2. Break eggs on top of the crabmeat and mix with sherry, salt, M.S.G., white pepper and scallion. Do not overbeat.

Put oil in hot skillet over high heat. Pour in egg mixture and turn the egg from edges to center. Turn constantly until the egg forms. Remove from heat and serve immediately.

This is a wonderful and easy dish to serve on fish days. You can get eggs from your refrigerator and canned crabmeat is easy to keep on hand or to buy at the store. Left-overs will be good to cook in fried rice.

4	**eggs**
2 TBS	**cooking oil**
1½ TBS	**soy sauce**
½ TBS	**sugar** — light brown sugar is better
¼ tsp	**M.S.G.**
2 TBS	**water**
1 TBS	**scallion** — minced (or onion)

Mix soy sauce, sugar, M.S.G., water in a small bowl.

Pour oil into hot skillet over medium high heat. Fry eggs two at a time. As soon as the edges of eggs are light brown and the whites are still soft, fold the eggs like a half-moon and the soft egg whites will hold the two edges together. Remove eggs to a plate when both sides of eggs are browned. Fry the remaining two eggs in the same manner.

Stir the minced scallion in the same skillet with the remaining oil. Return the fried and folded eggs and sprinkle the soy sauce mixture on the eggs. Mix well and serve hot.

This is a most easy and economical dish, a wonderful additional dish for your unexpected guests. If you prefer the egg yolk soft, then use high heat and cook less time.

荷包蛋

161

EGG FOO
YUNG
CANTONESE
STYLE

SERVINGS:
CHINESE 4-6
AMERICAN 2-3

笑
容
蛋

5		**eggs** — large (unbeaten)
½ cup		**cooked meat** — shredded — such as pork, beef, chicken, crabmeat (canned will be good), shrimp, etc. Left-over American roasted meat may be used.
½ cup		**celery** — shredded — no leaves
½ cup		**mushrooms** — shredded (fresh mushrooms, canned mushrooms — drained, or Chinese black mushrooms — softened and shredded)
1 cup		**bean sprouts** — fresh (less than ¼ lb) or bamboo shoots — shredded and drained
¼ cup		**onion** — shredded
1 tsp		**salt**
¼ tsp		**M.S.G.**
1 tsp		**dry sherry**
dash		**black pepper**
1 cup		**cooking oil** — for frying

Mix all the above ingredients, except oil, gently in a large bowl. (Do not beat the eggs.)

COOKING: Method 1 — Restaurant Way

Put ½ cup oil in hot *deep* skillet or Dutch oven (Chinese wock is suitable). Heat oil over a medium heat. Scoop ¼ of the egg mixture into the heated oil very carefully. Spoon the small pieces of egg on the large piece for trimming. When the edges of the large piece are brown, turn over gently and brown the other side. (For easy turning it is better to use two spoons or one spoon and one spatula.) Remove the cooked ones to a plate and fry the other 3 portions in the same manner. Add more oil when it is needed.

162

The oil in the skillet tends to foam. If the skillet is deep or you use a Dutch oven or Chinese wock, you can fry two portions at the same time.

Serve hot with or without the following sauce:

1 can	**chicken broth**
1 tsp	**catsup**
1 TBS	**soy sauce**
½ tsp	**salt**
2½ TBS	**flour** — mixed with ¼ cup cold water

Mix the above ingredients in a sauce pan. Cook the mixture over medium heat, stirring constantly. Bring to a boil until it thickens. Serve with the Egg Foo Yung in the same plate or in sauce bowl.

Below are some important principles for making this dish:

1. Never beat eggs, otherwise the ingredients will fall apart in the oil.

2. If you use the restaurant method, be careful of the bubbles from oil which are likely to overflow out of the pan. This is the reason I suggested using a deep skillet in the first place.

3. If any meat is to be added to the ingredients, it must be pre-cooked.

COOKING: Method 2 — Family Style

Put 4 TBS of oil in a hot skillet over medium heat. Add one-half of the mixture to skillet. Turn over and over in large sections until evenly cooked and golden brown on both sides. Remove and place on serving dish. Put 3 TBS more of oil in same skillet and cook the rest of the mixture in same manner. Serve hot with or without the sauce.

The restaurant method and family method have the same ingredients and preparation, except the family method uses less oil in cooking.

EGG	2	eggs
GARNISH	½ tsp	salt
	½ tsp	dry sherry
	¼ tsp	M.S.G.
	2 tsp	oil

Beat eggs with salt, dry sherry and M.S.G.

Put 1 tsp oil in hot skillet over medium heat. Spread it evenly with a small piece of kitchen paper towel. Pour in half of beaten egg, tipping skillet around so a thin layer barely covers the bottom. Cook until the edge is lightly browned and lifts out of the bottom (less than a minute). Remove to cutting board. Cut into four even strips. Pile the strips into layers and cut into very fine slivers. Using the remaining oil, cook the rest of the egg in the same way. This makes a nice garnish for salads, soups, and other dishes.

If the skillet is not well seasoned and the egg mixture sticks to the bottom, use a little more oil; but too much oil will not make a thin layer.

Vegetables

BUDDHISM IS ONE OF THE MAJOR RELIGIONS IN China. Many people of Buddhist faith eat only vegetables, things without life. Animal meat, seafood, eggs, anything with life, even some strong-smelling vegetables such as onion, garlic and scallion are "untouchable" to them. It is tradition that people eat only vegetables as a sacrifice for the faith on certain days, such as birthdays of important deities and their own birthdays (because their mothers were suffering on that day), or the day they go to pray at temples.

In China, the best vegetarian dishes are not served by restaurants but by some Buddhist temples. If you have the opportunity to enjoy a banquet prepared by these temples, I am sure you will be very much surprised by these fancy vegetarian dishes. Just like other banquets, they usually contain more than ten dishes. There are meat, chicken, duck or fish on the plate; however, they are made of flour, beans and vegetables. It is really amazing.

The refrigeration system is quite strange to most of Chinese stores and families. Many careful and elderly people eat only vegetables in summer to prevent any unhealthy effects.

If you are fortunate in having your own vegetable garden or live close to the country, you must know the pleasure of eating fresh-picked vegetables. The delicious taste and good texture of

165

these vegetables are worth the time worked in the garden or driving miles to buy them. After cooking, the fresh picked vegetables also have a kind of sweetness in taste. Sometimes we add a little bit of sugar (about 1 tsp) in cooking vegetables which are not fresh-picked, to improve the flavor.

In recent years, people started to notice that vegetable diet is good for health, especially for those who have high blood pressure and heart trouble. I think the best advantage of Chinese cooking is our combinations of vegetables and meats. They are both enriched in flavor. There are three major ways to cook vegetables. (It makes no difference what the vegetables are cooked with; by themselves, with meat or with other vegetables.)

1. Quick-stirring — to retain the pretty green color and good texture of vegetables as pea pods, green peppers, and tender part of cabbage. This is almost the only way to cook vegetables at restaurants. Never cover the pan or skillet while cooking.

2. Longer cooking — to cook those vegetables which are tough to chew or should be cooked soft such as carrot, winter melon, etc. Most of them are cooked by quick stirring first. As soon as the vegetable becomes translucent or gets too dry, then add ½ to 1 cup of water with the seasoning and simmer with cover on until tender, or add the seasoning later. Add more water if it gets dry again.

3. For salads — to prepare vegetables which can be eaten raw or can be served by cooking in a very short period such as radish, cucumber, asparagus, celery, etc. The vegetables should be parboiled or salted before mixing with the seasoning or dressing. Sesame seed oil and soy sauce are always used as salad dressing. Sometimes we use salt instead of soy sauce for retaining light, pretty color. Cooked meat, softened Japanese agar-agar, and egg garnish (see page 164) are often added to enrich the flavor and texture.

166

The following recipes are good, easy dishes and are suitable to serve here.

2	**cucumbers** — medium and narrow	
½ cup	**chicken shreds** — cooked	
¼ cup	**peanut butter**	
¼ cup	**water** — cold	
⅔ tsp	**salt**	
¼ tsp	**M.S.G.**	
1 TBS	**sesame seed oil**	

CUCUMBER SALAD WITH CHICKEN SHREDS

SERVINGS:
CHINESE 4-6
AMERICAN 2-3

1. Peel cucumbers, leaving some green underskin. Split down the middle, hollow out and discard the seedy portion. Cut diagonally in ¼-inch slices, making about 3 cups.

2. Tear the cooked and cooled chicken meat into shreds by the fingers. Left-over Cold Cut Chicken (page 106) and American roast chicken or turkey will be good to use.

3. Mix the peanut butter gradually with the ¼ cup water into a smooth paste in a small bowl. Add salt, M.S.G. and sesame seed oil. Set aside.

4. When time to serve, mix the cucumber slices with the peanut paste. Serve cold.

This is a heavier and fancier salad. Almost everybody likes it. In China we use sesame seed paste, but here only the Syrian Sesame Tahini is available. The Chinese sesame seed paste is browned before grinding and the Syrian Sesame Tahini is not browned so that they have different aroma. All of our Chinese here use peanut butter as a substitute. You may do the same, however, as it is easy to get.

If you like to try the Syrian Sesame Tahini, then omit the sesame seed oil.

167

PEKING SPINACH SALAD WITH MUSTARD DRESSING

4-6 SERVINGS

2 lb	**spinach** — loose is better — or 1 large package or 2 small packages
2 TBS	**dry mustard powder**
½ tsp	**vinegar**
1¼ tsp	**salt**
½ tsp	**M.S.G.**

1. Discard the yellow outer leaves of loose spinach (use stalks, too). Wash spinach carefully and drain.

2. Mix the mustard powder with 2 TBS cold water into a paste, then gradually add 2½ TBS cold water, vinegar, and ¼ tsp salt into the thin paste.

Put spinach into a large sauce pan with 6-8 cups of boiling water. Before the water boils again, drain the spinach through colander and soak the spinach in cold water long enough to cool and set the color. Drain it and squeeze the water out. Cut into fine pieces and place in a serving bowl. Mix with thin mustard paste the remaining 1 tsp salt and M.S.G. and serve cold.

This is a refreshing dish for the people who like hot dishes. In Peking, we especially use the older spinach with long stalks (almost 1 ft. long) as the stalk has better texture than the leaves. This is the reason the loose spinach is better. If you have a vegetable garden you may be interested in using the older spinach for this salad.

2-2½ lb **Chinese cabbage** or Chinese celery cabbage, 1 large or 2 medium heads
4 TBS **chicken fat** or cooking oil
1 tsp **sugar**
1½ tsp **salt**
½ TBS **corn starch**
¼ tsp **M.S.G.**

1. Discard the outer tough and yellow leaves. Wash the cabbage and cut stalks and leaves into 2-inch sections (split lengthwise the big and lower part of stalk for even pieces).

2. Mix corn starch with 2 TBS water.

Put chicken fat or oil in hot skillet. Add cabbage gradually to the skillet as much as can fit. When the cabbage is wilted, add ½ cup water, cover and simmer for 10 minutes or until tender. Stir occasionally. Mix in salt, sugar and M.S.G., then corn starch mixture. When it thickens, serve hot.

Cabbage heart cooked in chicken fat is a famous dish, and it is often served at banquets.

One to 2 TBS minced cooked Smithfield ham may be garnished for more coloring and flavor.

**SWEET
AND SOUR
RELISH**
(can be hot)

糖
醋
白
菜

1 head	**cabbage** — medium sized — about 2 lbs. or Chinese celery
½ TBS	**hot pepper flakes** — to your taste, as desired
½ cup	**light brown sugar**
⅓ cup	**cider vinegar**
2 TBS	**soy sauce**
2 tsp	**salt**
3 TBS	**cooking oil**

Cut cabbage in chunks, discarding core and tough outer leaves. Separate inner leaves. Mix pepper flakes, sugar, vinegar, soy sauce, and salt in a bowl and set aside.

Heat oil in large deep pan over medium heat. Add cabbage, stirring constantly until the small leaves have become transparent. Take care not to overcook, otherwise the cabbage will lose its crispness. Remove pan from heat and stir in the seasoning mixture. Pour the cabbage with the liquid into a large bowl. Bank cabbage around the edge of bowl, leaving a well in the center, so that it will cool evenly. Stir occasionally and rearrange as before until thoroughly cold.

This recipe is easy and very economical, and makes a wonderful side dish for people who like spicy food. This dish may be eaten warm, but it improves its flavor if chilled overnight, and may even be kept in refrigerator for several days.

2 bunches	**radishes** or 1 regular plastic bag	
½ tsp	**salt**	
2 TBS	**sugar** — light brown	
2 TBS	**cider vinegar**	
½ tsp	**sesame seed oil**	

1. Trim both ends of radish, wash and drain.

2. Crush the radishes gently by using the side of blade of cleaver or the bottom of a jar. Cut large ones in half.

3. Sprinkle ¼ tsp salt on the crushed radishes and let set for 15 minutes. Drain the liquid from radishes — about 1 tablespoon.

4. Mix the sugar with vinegar and pour over the radishes. Garnish with sesame seed oil and serve.

This dish is easy, requiring no cooking. Although the radishes will taste better by soaking longer in the sugar and vinegar, they will be discolored and less crisp.

If you like a hot dish, then ¼ tsp of hot pepper sauce may be added.

**BEAN
SPROUTS
SALAD
WITH EGG
GARNISH**

4-6 SERVINGS

蛋
絲
拌
豆
芽

1 lb	**raw bean sprouts** — about 4 cups packed tightly
2 TBS	**soy sauce**
1 tsp	**sesame seed oil**
¼ tsp	**M.S.G.**

egg garnish

Prepare the egg garnish as on page 164.

Mix soy sauce, sesame seed oil and M.S.G. in a bowl and set aside.

Add the bean sprouts to a large sauce pan with 10 cups or more of boiling water over high heat. Before the water boils again, remove pan from heat and pour and drain the bean sprouts with boiling water in a colander. Then soak (or rinse evenly) the bean sprouts in cold water until thoroughly cold. Drain very well.

Put the drained bean sprouts in a large salad bowl and add the egg garnish on the top. Cover and store in refrigerator until ready to serve. When it is time to serve, mix in the soy sauce mixture.

This is a summer dish in China. Since Americans are familiar with bean sprouts and have learned to grow them at home (page 52), I think this is an easy good dish for you.

To retain the crisp and sweet taste of bean sprouts, the bean sprouts should be removed before water boils again and cooled immediately and thoroughly.

Shredded cooked chicken and pork may be added with egg garnish. Shredded pea pods may be parboiled and added to the bean sprouts for more color.

172

1 10 oz. pkg	**fresh spinach** – or 1 lb loose fresh spinach	
2 TBS	**cooking oil**	
½ tsp	**salt**	
1 tsp	**sugar**	

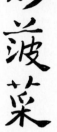

Wash spinach thoroughly, even if packed, and drain well. Put oil and salt in a hot skillet or deeper pan over a high heat. Add spinach first, then sugar. Stir and cook for about 1 to 2 minutes until the spinach is well wilted. Spread flat on a plate and serve hot.

This spinach goes well with Shanghai duck, Shanghai ham, or other dishes cooked with a large amount of soy sauce. Serve separately or put it around or under any one of these meat dishes. Drain if too watery.

In China we have only the loose spinach in the market. We are all fond of the sweet taste of fresh spinach in late fall, especially with the pink root. We scrape the root with the fingernail and leave it about ½-inch attached to the spinach stalk. The pink root with the green stalk leaves is so pretty. Poets describe this as the red-mouthed green parrot. Sometimes I go especially with my children to a nearby farm and get the owner's permission to dig the spinach this way.

Beet tops and mustard greens can be cooked in the same way. They just need a little longer cooking, about 5 minutes, and add a little water, 3-4 TBS, when the liquid of vegetables is dried out while cooking.

MUSHROOMS WITH BEAN CURD

3-5 SERVINGS

香菇豆腐

1 can	**French mushrooms,** 4 oz, or fresh mushrooms — about 2 cups sliced 4″ to 5″
4 small cakes	**bean curd** or a large square
2 TBS	**cooking oil**
1 tsp	**salt**
1 TBS	**soy sauce**
¼ tsp	**M.S.G.**
½ TBS	**corn starch**

1. Drain the canned French mushrooms and save the liquid, about ½ cup.

2. Cut the bean curd cakes into 8 pieces, about ½″ x 1″.

3. Mix the corn starch with ½ cup liquid from the can.

Put the oil in hot skillet over medium heat. Add mushrooms, stir for 2 minutes, then add the bean curd. Add the salt, soy sauce, and M.S.G., stir and cook for another 3 minutes. When the liquid from bean curd is almost dry, stir in the corn starch mixture until it thickens. Serve hot.

You may garnish with 1 tsp sesame seed oil.

This dish has been greatly liked by many vegetarians, notably Prof. Norbert Wiener of M.I.T. who spent a long time in Peking. Bean curd is obtainable in China-town (see shopping list). Canned bean curd has not been widely used as yet.

It may be purchased in small cakes or large cakes (they will cut as much as you need).

A few pea pods may be added for coloring. Cook the pea pods before the mushrooms. Remove the pods, then cook the mushrooms in the same skillet.

1 small bunch	**fresh asparagus**	
3 TBS	**soy sauce**	
¼ tsp	**M.S.G.**	
1 tsp	**sesame seed oil**	

Cut off the white and tough part of asparagus and remove the lower little leaves (sometimes there is sand there). Wash and drain. Rolling-cut the asparagus into 1½″ lengths (see page 29).

Parboil the asparagus pieces by plunging in 6 cups of boiling water in a sauce pan over high heat. When the water boils again, drain and plunge into cold water until the asparagus is thoroughly cold. Drain well.

When it is time to serve, mix the asparagus with the soy sauce and M.S.G. Garnish with sesame seed oil.

1 lb	**green beans**	
2 TBS	**cooking oil**	
1 tsp	**salt**	
1 tsp	**sugar**	

GREEN BEANS

3-4 SERVINGS

String the beans and break in half, (if very long, into three). Wash and drain.

Put the oil in a deep skillet or sauce pan (not hot) over medium heat. Add the beans and stir frequently. As soon as the beans turn to darker green add ½ cup water. Cover and simmer for 10 to 15 minutes until tender (10 minutes for firm tender, 15 minutes for soft tender). Put salt and sugar and cook without cover for 1 minute. Serve hot.

Green beans tend to splatter in oil, so I suggest using a deeper pan, and starting to cook in an unheated skillet or sauce pan for less oil spatter.

175

CELERY SALAD	½ bunch	**large celery** without leaves — fine shreds — about 4 cups
4-6 SERVINGS	1	**carrot** — fine shreds — about 1 cup
	1 TBS	**ginger root** — peeled and shredded fine — optional
	2 tsp	**salt**
	3 TBS	**soy sauce**
	¼ tsp	**M.S.G.**
	1 tsp	**sesame seed oil**

拌芹菜

Soak the celery, carrot and ginger shreds in ice water with 2 tsp salt for ½ hour (no more than 1 hour) and drain. Cover and store in refrigerator until ready to serve.

When time to serve, mix the soy sauce and M.S.G. and garnish with sesame seed oil.

Never add the soy sauce too long before serving as the soy sauce will stain the vegetables.

Cooked chicken shreds may be added.

1 medium head	**cauliflower** — about 1 lb of the flowerets	**CAULIFLOWER**
2 TBS	**cooking oil**	4-6 SERVINGS
1 tsp	**salt**	
¼ tsp	**M.S.G.**	
1 tsp	**corn starch**	

1. Cut the cauliflower from the stem end into flowerets about 1½ to 2 inches long and ½ inch wide.

2. Mix the corn starch with 2 TBS cold water, and set aside.

Pour oil in a sauce pan over a medium heat. Add cauliflower and stir for 2 minutes. Add ½ cup water into sauce pan, cover and simmer for 10 minutes. Mix in the salt and M.S.G., then add the well-stirred corn starch mixture. After a few stirrings, the liquid is thickened. Serve hot.

Since many Americans serve raw cauliflower for cocktails do not be afraid if the cauliflower is under-cooked. Just reach the tenderness you desire; 10 minutes simmering will make it firm and tender, 15 minutes will make it soft. If you like crisp cauliflower then do not simmer.

You may garnish with 2 TBS minced cooked Smithfield ham to add more flavor and color.

MUSHROOMS, BAMBOO SHOOTS AND PEA PODS

3-4 SERVINGS

½ lb	**pea pods**
½ cup	**bamboo shoots** — sliced and rinsed
½ cup	**dried black mushrooms**
½ tsp	**salt**
2 TBS	**soy sauce**
1 tsp	**sugar**
¼ tsp	**M.S.G.**
4 TBS	**cooking oil**

String the pea pods, rinse and pat dry with kitchen towel. Soak black mushrooms in boiling water and cover for 15 minutes until soft. Squeeze out water, cut off stems and cut each into 2 or 4 sections.

Put 2 TBS oil in hot skillet over a high heat. Add salt first and then pea pods, stirring constantly until the pods turn darker green (less than 1 minute). Remove pods and spread out on a plate. In the same skillet, add the remaining 2 TBS oil. Stir in bamboo shoots and mushrooms, then add soy sauce, sugar, and M.S.G. Stir and cook for 3 minutes. Mix in the cooked pea pods and serve immediately.

Fried Rice

THE WAY OF SERVING FRIED RICE IN CHINA IS SO
different from here. In China fried rice is a way
to warm cold cooked rice for somebody late for
mealtime or the unexpected friend who drops in
when the family meal is just over. The fried rice
is flavored so that no main dish is needed; just a simple soup will
be enough. We never serve fried rice at a party or order it at an
exclusive restaurant. The fried rice is only served at street corner
food stands or small restaurants. Here at our restaurant Chinese
or oriental people never order fried rice with their meal; they
prefer plain boiled rice. Almost every American has fried rice
with other dishes, except for gourmets who specialize in Chinese
foods.

Many Americans blame themselves for not being able to
cook fried rice dry and fluffy. Fluffy fried rice depends on fluffy
plain boiled rice. Since you already know how to cook perfect
rice (See page 40), making fried rice fluffy is no problem at all.
The following rules are a must for fluffy fried rice:

1. The cooked rice being used for fried rice must be fluffy
and dry (only long grain rice should be used).

2. No soy sauce (but a little can be used if rice is hard or
dry), gravy from cooked meat, or any liquid should be added.

3. While cooking, the fried rice must be stirred constantly
and the grains must be separated and heated thoroughly. To

179

re-heat fried rice, do in the same cooking manner by stirring constantly; if too dry sprinkle with 2-3 TBS water. Never heat it in the oven, or the rice will be hard along the edges of container.

If you cook plain boiled rice especially for making fried rice, it is not necessary to wait for the just cooked rice to be very cold, or to cook rice the day before. As soon as the cooked rice is cool enough so it is firm, then it would be all right to make fried rice. Actually the grains will separate more easily if the rice is warm.

EGG FRIED RICE, HOME STYLE

3-5 SERVINGS

蛋
炒
飯

4 cups	**cooked rice** — warm or cold
2 tsp	**salt**
2-3	**eggs**
½ tsp	**M.S.G.**
½ tsp	**dry sherry**
1 TBS	**scallion** — minced
4 TBS	**cooking oil or bacon dripping**

Put cooked rice in a large bowl. Break eggs on rice and add other ingredients except oil. Mix thoroughly with wooden spoon or hands and break the rice lumps.

Place oil in hot skillet over medium high heat. Add rice mixture and stir constantly for 8-10 minutes. At first it will stick together, but as it cooks the grains separate.

This is the authentic fried rice in most parts of China. In China we call it egg fried rice; my children call it golden rice. I mix the eggs with the cooked rice, before cooking, to make it easier in separating the grains and coating evenly with eggs.

2 or 3	**eggs**	*FRIED RICE,* *CANTONESE* *STYLE* 3-5 SERVINGS
2 tsp	**salt**	
½ tsp	**M.S.G.**	
½ tsp	**dry sherry**	
2 TBS	**onion** — minced	
5 TBS	**cooking oil**	
4 cups	**cooked rice** — warm or cold	
1 tsp	**Chinese brown gravy syrup** or ½ tsp Kitchen Bouquet or Gravy Master	
1 cup	**bean sprouts** — or the shredded thick part of lettuce as a substitute.	

Beat eggs with salt, M.S.G. and sherry.

Pour oil in hot skillet over medium high heat. Stir in minced onion and then the egg mixture. Scramble and break into small pieces until quite dry. Add rice, brown syrup, and bean sprouts. Stir constantly until the ingredients are well blended and thoroughly heated — about 8 to 10 minutes.

One-half cup diced or shredded *cooked* meat may be added with the rice, if desired, such as pork, ham, chicken, shrimp, or beef. Left-over from your American roasted meat would be good to use. (Roast lamb is not suitable as it has a strong flavor.)

This kind of fried rice is served in Chinese restaurants here. Different kinds of cooked meat can be added, pork to make pork fried rice or shrimp for shrimp fried rice, etc. Brown gravy syrup makes the fried rice brown, or Kitchen Bouquet or Gravy Master can be used as a substitute. Never use soy sauce unless the rice is very dry or you prefer your fried rice soft.

CHOO CHOO
TRAIN
FRIED RICE

3-5 SERVINGS

火
車
蛋
炒
飯

2 or 3	**eggs**
½ tsp	**M.S.G.**
½ tsp	**dry sherry**
2 TBS	**onion** — minced
4 TBS	**cooking oil**
4 cups	**cooked rice** warm or cold
1 ½ tsp	**salt**
½ cup	**ham** — diced
½ cup	**green peas** — parboiled or frozen green peas are good

Beat eggs with M.S.G. and sherry.

Pour oil in hot skillet over medium high heat. Stir in minced onion and the beaten eggs. Scramble the eggs into small pieces. Add rice, salt, ham and peas, and stir constantly for 8 to 10 minutes until the ingredients are well blended and heated.

This fried rice is usually served on dining coaches in China. Green peas, diced ham and yellow eggs are so pretty with white rice. Every Chinese who travels a lot knows what the train egg fried rice is. I called it Choo Choo train fried rice to my children when they were young; they ate it better with this name.

182

Chinese Noodles

NOODLES ARE A STAPLE FOOD IN CHINA, ESPECIALLY to the Northern Chinese; rice is more important to the Southern Chinese. Noodles can be cooked plain and served with sauce as Peking Meat Sauce Noodles, or recooked or reheated and served in soups as Chinese Noodles in Soup for a whole meal.

Fried Noodles are often served as a simple lunch or a snack in the afternoon or midnight. Chinese Noodles in Soup is also served for that purpose.

The noodles in this book are cooked the most famous ways. Different meats, leafy vegetables or pickled vegetables may be used to suit the taste and convenience.

Regardless of how the noodles are served, in dry form from packages or soft freshly made, they must be cooked in boiling water for a few minutes (about 3-10 minutes for dried noodles and 1-2 minutes for freshly made noodles), and rinsed of excess starch and then drained before serving, adding to or cooking with other ingredients.

I specified the different make of noodles to use in certain dishes for best results and authentic flavor and appearance. If you like to make the noodles at home, see page 199 which is best for use in soup, and the results will delight a Chinese gourmet.

The noodles should be cooked thoroughly and soft but still have a smooth texture. Never over-cook them or let them stay in

183

soup too long as they will be too soft and messy. After the noodles are plain cooked and waiting for the time to serve, then rinse thoroughly in cold water, drain very well and mix with 1 TBS cooking oil to prevent them from sticking together. Left-overs should be stored in a plastic bag or covered tightly to avoid dry edges. Also, dried noodles can be cooked a day ahead in this manner.

In China noodles are always served on birthdays like American birthday cakes (many Chinese also serve cakes). In China long life is the most important good fortune; the noodle is long and symbolizes long life. We celebrate the older generation's birthdays very seriously with big parties; especially the tenth anniversaries such as forty, fifty, etc. (sometimes also for ninths such as 39, 49, etc. for good luck). The older one is, the bigger the party. Children's birthdays are just family affairs or with close relatives.

At birthday banquets there is always a noodle dish and steamed rolls in a peach shape (peach is another symbol of long life).

PEKING MEAT SAUCE NOODLES

4-6 SERVINGS

炸
醬
麵

1 lb pkg	**spaghetti** — thin or regular
Sauce:	
1 cup	**ground pork**
1 tsp	**dry sherry**
½ cup	**scallion** — minced
⅔ cup	**bean paste** — see page 21
1 TBS	**Hoi Sin sauce** — optional
2 TBS	**soy sauce**
¼ tsp	**M.S.G.**
1 TBS	**cooking oil**

184

Serve with:

1 bunch **radishes** — shredded with skin, about 1 cup

½ **cucumber** — shredded, peeled, seeded — about 1 cup

1½ cups **raw bean sprouts** — parboiled and drained

½-10 oz. pkg **spinach** — parboiled. Squeeze out water and cut into fine pieces about ½″ long.

3 or 4 cloves **garlic** — skinned and minced

1. Prepare the vegetables which are served with noodles as specified above.

2. Mix pork with sherry.

3. Mix the bean paste, Hoi Sin sauce, soy sauce and M.S.G. in a small bowl.

Cook the spaghetti in a large pot with at least 10 cups of boiling water. Stir the spaghetti in the water and bring to a boil. Cook over a low heat for 10 minutes (stir occasionally from bottom). Cook without cover or leave the cover open a little as the liquid will overflow if it is tightly covered. After it is cooked, cover the pot and let stay for 5 minutes. Rinse the cooked spaghetti (about 10 cups) in colander with hot water. Drain and serve hot with the sauce and vegetables.

While the spaghetti is cooking, cook the sauce:

Put the oil in a deep hot skillet or sauce pan over medium heat. Stir in the ground pork for 1 minute and then the minced scallions. Cook for another 1 minute. Add the mixed bean paste, and after a few stirrings add ⅔ cup water and cook over *low* heat for less than 2 minutes making a thin sauce. Put in a small bowl and serve on the table with spaghetti and vegetables.

Mix the spaghetti with sauce (about ¼ cup sauce to 1½ cups spaghetti) and vegetables, (about 1 TBS each kind) and ¼ tsp garlic (if desired). Serve in a deep plate or individual bowls. Usually people eat more of this kind noodles, about 1½-3 cups cooked spaghetti for one serving. If you are serving to a smaller party, then reduce the amount to half or as you need.

This is the most well-known noodle dish from Peking. The best noodles to serve in this dish are pulled and stretched by hand from a very stiff and elastic dough. This kind of noodle is very smooth and chewy. The spaghetti here is closest to it.

I compare Peking Meat Sauce Noodles to Italian spaghetti with meat sauce. I feel strongly that Marco Polo brought this recipe home from China in the thirteenth century. It is an old, good dish and widely beloved by Chinese, Japanese, and Koreans because the process of making it is easy and economical. Sometimes I serve this dish to a gathering of as many as two hundred Chinese friends.

1 lb	**dried egg noodles**
9 TBS	**cooking oil**
1 cup	**meat** — shredded
3 cups	**cabbage** — shredded
1 cup	**canned bamboo shoots** — shredded
1 cup	**fresh mushrooms** — sliced or Chinese dried mushrooms — softened and shredded.
1 tsp	**dry sherry**
2½ TBS	**corn starch** (½ TBS to mix with pork)
3 tsp	**salt**
1½ cups	**stock or water**
½ tsp	**M.S.G.**

*CHINESE
FRIED
NOODLES —
BOTH SIDES
GOLDEN*

4-6 SERVINGS

1. Place egg noodles in boiling water. Cover and cook over very low heat or cover loosely so the water will not overflow until soft (about 3 min). Stir from bottom occasionally. Then rinse with cold water and drain.

2. Mix the cooked noodles with 2 TBS oil to prevent the noodles from sticking together. Set aside until ready to fry.

3. Mix the shredded meat with sherry and ½ TBS corn starch.

4. Mix the remaining 2 TBS corn starch with ½ cup water or stock.

Noodles —

Heat 5 TBS oil in large skillet. Add greased noodles, flattening them evenly to make a cake. If the skillet is not very large then divide into two cakes.

Fry over medium high heat until the bottom is golden brown, then turn over to brown the other side. Keep the

187

browned noodle cake in warm oven while cooking the sauce (or cook both at the same time).

Sauce —

Heat 2 TBS oil and the salt in skillet over medium high heat. Stir in meat mixture and cook about 2 minutes.

Add cabbage, mushrooms, bamboo shoots and the remaining cup of water or stock. Cook until tender, stirring constantly.

Mix in the corn starch mixture and then add the M.S.G. When liquid has thickened pour over noodle cake and serve immediately.

This kind of fried noodle (actually pan-fried) is in its most fancy and tasty form. In China it is a treat to serve fried noodles in this way. With the convenience of using ovens here, you can make them in same skillet, first noodles then the sauce.

CHINESE NOODLES — SOFT FRIED

4-6 SERVINGS

炒
麵

½ lb	**dried fine egg noodles** or thin spaghetti or homemade noodles
½ cup	**pork** — shredded
½ cup	**bamboo shoots** — shredded
½ cup	**black mushrooms** — softened and shredded
2 cups	**Chinese celery cabbage** — shredded
1 tsp	**dry sherry**
1 tsp	**corn starch**
4 TBS	**cooking oil**
2 TBS	**soy sauce**
1 tsp	**salt**
½ tsp	**M.S.G.**
¼ lb	**raw bean sprouts** — about 1 cup tightly packed (optional)
¼ pkg	**spinach** — a 10 oz. package rinsed and drained (optional)

1. Cook and prepare the noodles as above recipe (page 187).

2. Mix the pork with sherry and corn starch.

Put the oil in a large skillet over medium heat. Add the mixed pork and stir for 1 minute. Put the bamboo shoots, black mushrooms and cabbage in the skillet. Cook until the cabbage is wilted. Mix in the soy sauce, salt and M.S.G. Add cooked noodles and after a few stirrings put in the bean sprouts and/or spinach. Turn and stir constantly for even flavor. When the noodles are heated thoroughly, about 3 minutes, and the bean sprouts and spinach are also wilted, then remove the noodles to a large platter. Serve hot. Vinegar and ketchup may be mixed with noodles for individual tastes.

The noodles in this dish should be smooth and not very soft, otherwise it will be messy. The flat and wide noodles from the Chinese noodle factory are very soft after plain cooked in water, so they are not suitable for use in this dish. Only steamed flat and wide noodles can be used as they are cooked just by dipping in boiling water to soften a little.

CHINESE
NOODLES
IN SOUP

3-5 servings

½ lb   **dried fine egg noodles,** or 1 lb. soft freshly made noodles from Chinese noodle factory, or home made noodles. (See page 199).

½ cup   **pork** — shredded

½ cup   **bamboo shoots** — shredded

½ cup   **dried black mushrooms** — softened and shredded

2 cups   **Chinese celery cabbage** — shredded

1 tsp   **dry sherry**

1 tsp   **corn starch**

1 can   **chicken broth**

1½ tsp   **salt,** or 1 tsp salt with 1 TBS soy sauce

¼ tsp   **M.S.G.**

1 TBS   **cooking oil**

1. Cook the dried egg noodles in a large sauce pan with at least 6 cups of boiling water. Cook over low heat without cover for 3 minutes for dried noodles (1 minute for fresh soft noodles) and stir occasionally from the bottom to avoid sticking. Rinse the noodles thoroughly in a colander with cold water. Drain well.

2. Mix the meat with sherry and corn starch.

Put the oil in a large sauce pan over medium heat. Stir in the mixed pork for 1 minute and then the cabbage, bamboo shoots and mushrooms. Cook and stir until the cabbage is wilted. Add chicken broth, salt, M.S.G. and 4 cups water. Bring to a boil. Put the cooked and drained noodles in the sauce pan with the soup. When the soup boils again, remove from heat.

Divide the noodles into 3 to 5 individual big bowls with soup and place the cooked shreds on top of the

190

noodles. (The meat and vegetables always settle to the bottom of the pan.) Serve immediately.

The above ingredients are commonly used with noodles. Chicken meat and shrimp meat may be used instead of pork. Wood ears and golden needles may replace the mushrooms and bamboo shoots. Sometimes just the pork and cabbage are used. The noodles will swell and become very soft if they are soaked in liquid, so prompt serving is essential. Do not put the noodles in the soup until it is time to serve. If it is a long waiting time, then mix the cooked noodles with 1 TBS cooking oil to prevent them from sticking together.

Some people do not cook the noodles again in the soup; they just put the plain cooked noodles in the bowl and pour the soup over the noodles. You may do this if the noodles are served to a large party or if the noodles are very soft. (Be sure the cooked noodles are warm or rinse them again in hot water.)

Desserts

THE IDEA OF SERVING DESSERT AT THE END OF A meal used to be strange to Chinese people. Even at present time, dessert is not very popular in China. We only use dessert at banquet dinners where it is served between main dishes. The dessert, which may contain more than one item, is served hot (only in summer served cold occasionally). In wealthy families, they use sweet and salty pastry or noodles as afternoon snacks. Many of the pastries and desserts require much work and time to prepare. I do not think you should be bothered with them now as even most Chinese do not make them in this country.

The following recipes are enjoyed by many participants of my cooking classes. If you are too busy to prepare any dessert, simply serve Chinese preserved fruit pierced with toothpicks, canned lichee nuts and/or mandarin oranges in a bowl with syrup. It will delight your guests. Use fortune cookies from a Chinese grocer; they add lots of fun.

After a Chinese meal, a cup of hot tea is more enjoyable than dessert. Light dessert is preferred at Chinese dinners, and fresh fruit is the best. Fresh fruit on a plate can be used as a centerpiece on the dining table also.

192

1 envelope	**unflavored gelatine** (or 1 TBS)
⅓ cup	**cold water**
¾ cup	**boiling water**
⅓ cup	**sugar**
1 cup	**milk** (homogenized)
1 tsp	**almond extract**
	food coloring
	fruit and syrup
	mint garnish

杏仁豆腐

1. Soften gelatine in ⅓ cup cold water. Add ¾ cup boiling water and sugar. Stir until thoroughly dissolved. Pour in milk and extract, or food coloring (to shade desired). Mix well. Put in cake pan and chill until set.

2. Cut in ½ inch cubes and serve with fruits and syrup such as canned Mandarin oranges, fruit cocktail, sliced peaches, or fresh strawberries. Garnish with mint leaves which will make it more colorful.

There is not enough syrup from the canned fruit, and no syrup with fresh fruits. So mix ⅓ cup sugar with 2 cups of water and ½ tsp almond extract and chill. Add to fruit and almond float as desired.

Originally from Peking, this is a widely welcomed summer banquet dessert. In China we use the Japanese agar-agar and grind raw blanched almonds into a kind of milk which makes the flavor and whiteness. Here, I use gelatine instead, as well as milk and almond extract, which are much easier to handle and give about the same result.

The original Almond Float is without any fruit; just sugar water is added so that it can float. I have added Mandarin oranges to it since we first opened the restaurant. I believe the Mandarin orange not only enriches the flavor and color but also gives an oriental feeling as it is imported from Japan. The colors especially match our restaurant. I have been delighted to give out this recipe to many customers by their request, and they are pleased with the result.

Almond Float also makes a wonderful drink to serve at parties as punch; just add more liquid and cut the almond gelatine into finer pieces.

Once I added a few drops of green coloring in the almond gelatine and served with Mandarin oranges. Everybody was delighted to see the pretty colors. Since then, I use different colors with different fruits and it seems like a new dessert everytime. Pink with strawberry; light yellow or light green with peach or orange—you may select the coloring you wish.

ALMOND TEA

4-6 SERVINGS

⅔ cup	**cooked rice** — left-over boiled rice is good. short grain rice is smoother.
2 TBS	**almond paste**
4 cups	**water**
1 tsp	**almond extract**
⅓ cup	**white sugar**

Golden brown sugar for garnish

杏仁茶

Blend cooked rice, almond paste, and ½ cup water in blender at low speed for 5 minutes. Then add ½ cup water a little at a time until rice is blended into a very smooth thin paste.

Remove the paste to a large sauce pan. Use the remaining water to rinse blender (one cup at a time) and pour the liquid into the same pan. Blend the liquid very well with an egg beater or put it through strainer.

Cook the liquid over medium heat, stirring constantly until it comes to a boil (never cover the pan). Mix in almond extract and sugar. Serve hot in tea cups, or small bowls, or rice bowls. Sprinkle with 1 tsp golden brown sugar per cup for garnish and decoration.

In China we used to grind soaked raw rice and almond to make the almond tea. As I can remember, vendors sold hot almond tea from door to door in the morning, afternoon and evening. It is a wonderful drink on cold days. Now I have improved this old method by using cooked rice instead of soaked raw rice — thanks to Mrs. Helen Hensick's question: *Mrs. Chen, can we use cooked rice?* After I tried a few times, I arrived at this recipe.

Almond tea is also very good to serve as a hot drink after outings on cold days such as football games, etc. It fills and warms the stomach and gives you time to prepare supper.

ALMOND TEA — NO. 2
4-6 SERVINGS

Rice flour is available at Chinese groceries in 1 lb. packages. Sometimes it is also available at special food stores. If you can get it fresh, not stale (tell by sniffing) then use this recipe:

⅓ cup	rice flour
2 TBS	almond paste
4 cups	water
⅓ cup	sugar
1 tsp	almond extract

Golden brown sugar for garnish.

Mix the rice flour and almond paste in a sauce pan with ½ cup of cold water, stirring into a very smooth paste. Gradually add the remaining water.

Put the sauce pan over medium heat and stir the liquid constantly until it boils. Add sugar, almond extract, and serve in cups or bowls. Garnish with golden brown sugar (½ to 1 tsp).

This is the easier way to make almond tea, but the problem is the rice flour must be fresh, otherwise the flavor will be spoiled. Many Chinese are using corn starch instead of rice here. To me it is much different since I had this so often in Peking when I was a young girl.

ORANGE TAPIOCA CHINESE STYLE

6-8 SERVINGS

4 oz	**large tapioca pearls** — about ½ heaping cup
⅓ cup	**granulated sugar**
1 can	**Mandarin oranges** — 11 oz

Soak the tapioca in 2 cups of cold water for at least 4 hours or overnight.

Pour the tapioca with the water into a sauce pan and add another 2 cups of water. Bring to a boil, cover and simmer for ½ hour over very low heat. Remove sauce pan from the heat and set for 15 minutes, then the tapioca will turn to transparent entirely.

Add the sugar and Mandarin oranges to the sauce pan and bring to a boil again. Serve hot.

This is a dessert which is often served at banquets. You may use a fresh orange, peeled, with membrane and seed removed instead of canned Mandarin oranges as is the old original way.

STEAMED EGG CAKE

3	**large eggs** or 4 medium eggs
½ tsp	**vanilla extract**
⅓ cup	**water**
1 cup	**flour**
¼ tsp	**baking powder**
1¼ cup	**sugar**
10 drops	**yellow food coloring** (optional)
1 TBS	**colored sugar** (optional)

1. Separate egg whites and yolks. Beat egg whites until stiff but not dry.

2. Beat yolks slightly with vanilla and water.

3. Sift flour with baking powder first, then again with the sugar.

4. Line bottom and sides of 8″ round pan with wax paper or aluminum foil.

5. Start heating water in steamer which must be big enough to fit in the 8″ round pan.

6. Mix sifted flour, baking powder, and sugar into egg yolk mixture and stir in coloring.

7. Fold in beaten egg whites to the batter.

8. Pour batter into prepared pan and rap pan sharply on the table several times to remove large air bubbles.

Place pan on rack two inches above boiling water in steamer (see page 34) and steam over medium high heat for 20 to 25 minutes until inserted toothpick comes out clean.

When cake is done, cover pan with large round plate (at least 9″) and turn upside down so that the cake is on the plate. Pull off paper and turn cake right side up. Decorate with sparkling colored sugar. Serve hot or cold. Hot is better.

This cake is good for the person on a low fat diet. As I mentioned before, since an oven is not common in Chinese families, steaming is the method used. Here is a good way to avoid heating up the kitchen in Summer.

PEA JELLY	1 lb	split peas
SQUARE	1½ cups	granulated sugar
12 SERVINGS	1 TBS	plain gelatine
	few drops	green food coloring (if desired)

whipped cream and candied or maraschino cherries (optional)

1. Soak the split peas in 6 cups or more of water overnight. Drain.
2. Soften the gelatine in ½ cup of cold water.

豌
豆
黄

Put the drained swelled peas in a pressure cooker with 5 cups of water. Bring to a boil and cook over very low heat with the pressure cap for 1 hour until very, very soft. Strain the cooked peas into a sauce pan. Mix well with sugar, softened gelatine and green food coloring. Pour the mixed peas into an oblong roasting pan to set in refrigerator for a few hours. Cut the pea jelly into squares and serve cold. You may decorate with whipped cream and red candied or maraschino cherries for dessert.

If you serve to a smaller party, then reduce the amounts of half.

In China we use many kinds of beans and peas in dessert or pastry fillings. People in Peking like Pea Jelly Square very much, particularly in summer. Usually they eat it at the afternoon tea break or as candy (rather than as a dessert). In China we do not add green coloring so that the color is rather more close to yellow than green. If the green coloring is added and decorated with whipped cream and red cherry, it will be most ideal to serve at Christmas and even on St. Patrick's day.

Serve this dessert to the people who had been in Peking for a long time. They will be delighted to have this again. Probably they will ask for seconds.

How To Make Noodles, Egg Roll And Wonton Skins At Home

SINCE THERE ARE ONLY A FEW CHINATOWNS, A noodle factory is not always available. It is important that you know how to make egg roll and wonton skins at home. Although you can get noodles at most markets, this recipe for noodles is excellent.

2 cups	**flour**
1	**egg or egg white**
1/3 cup	**cold water**

Beat the egg with water and add to flour. Stir thoroughly until well mixed. Knead for about 5 minutes into a stiff dough. Cover dough with a damp cloth and let set for at least ½ hour.

This dough should be very stiff and after covering with the damp cloth the dough will be more smooth and softened a little. Since the dryness of the flour is influenced by the humidity of the weather, sometimes the flour has to be kept in a very dry place or it will not form together. You must then wet your hands, shaking off the excess water, and knead until the dough forms together. You may wet your hands for a second time but never over three times.

Put about 1 cup dry corn starch in a clean handkerchief or two layers of cheese cloth, tightening with string to flour the board and dough. See fig. 2.

If making noodles then divide the dough into four equal parts and form each into a round cake.

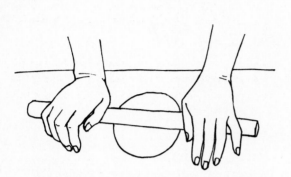

FIG. 1   Roll each cake into a flat pancake about 7″ in diameter.

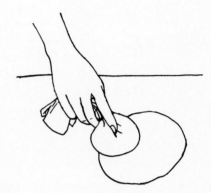

FIG. 2   Flouring the board and dough as needed to prevent sticking.

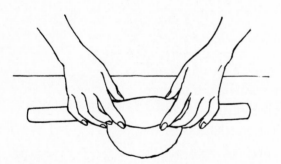

FIG. 3   Flour these pancakes lightly and roll up evenly on the roller

Some times the ordinary roller is not long enough for this work. Get a hardwood 1-inch dowel about 18 inches long to use as a roller.

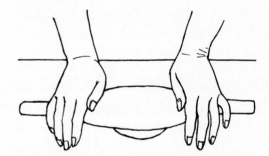

FIG. 4   Roll out the pancakes on the roller, kneading down heavily but evenly since the dough is stiff

Unroll the flat cake, flour and roll up again (change the edges). Repeat until the flat cake is very thin about 12″ in diameter.

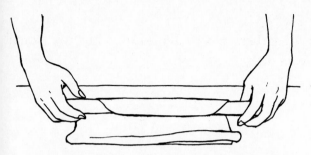

FIG. 5 Flour both sides and roll up on the roller again. Now unroll in folds about 2″ wide.

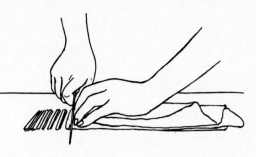

FIG. 6 Using a sharp knife, shred straightly across these folds into about 1/16 inch wide even strips. Be sure to cut all the way through.

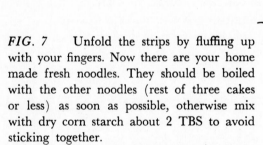

FIG. 7 Unfold the strips by fluffing up with your fingers. Now there are your home made fresh noodles. They should be boiled with the other noodles (rest of three cakes or less) as soon as possible, otherwise mix with dry corn starch about 2 TBS to avoid sticking together.

Continue to make noodles with other three cakes in same manner.

To make egg roll and wonton skins, divide the dough into 6 pieces and follow the same procedure as for noodles. Roll out also to 12 inches in diameter which will make the skins thinner than the noodles.

EGG ROLL & WONTON SKINS

FIG. 8 Check and roll the edges into even thickness.

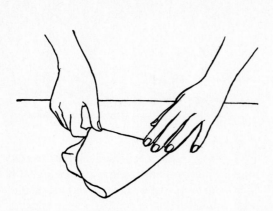

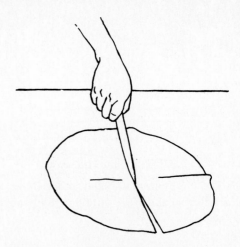

FIG. 9   Now fold one half over on the other. Fold again to form four quadrants.

FIG. 10   Using a sharp knife, cut along the folds into four quadrants. These are egg roll skins. Repeat with other cakes to make 24 pieces egg roll skins.

If you cut the thin cake into three even strips and again cut across into nine even squares they are wonton skins.

Ready-made egg roll skins from a Chinese noodle factory are much easier to use. See page 219 for more information.

How To Make Mandarin Pancakes
And Eat In Proper Way

The Mandarin thin pancake is one of the popular foods in Peking. It is served with famous Peking Duck and some meat, egg and vegetable dishes such as Moo Shi Pork.

1¾ cup	**flour** such as Pillsbury or King Arthur
¾ cup	**boiling water**
2 tsp	**sesame seed oil or cooking oil**

Mix flour and boiling water in a bowl with wooden spoon or chopsticks. As soon as your hands can stand the heat, knead the hot dough smoothly together. Knead for 3 minutes then cover with a wet towel and set aside for at least ½ hour.

FIG. 1   Form the dough with your hands into a cylinder about 12 inches long.

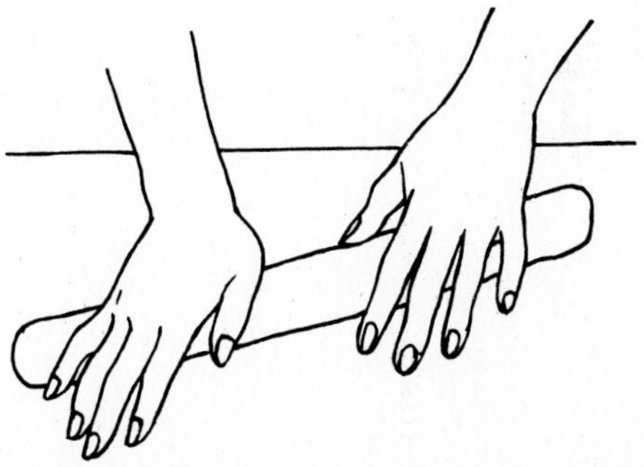

FIG. 2   Roll it evenly on a lightly floured board. And make the big strip exactly 12″ long.

203

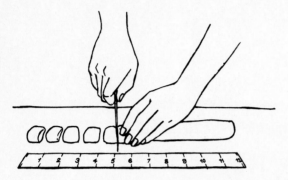

FIG. 3   Now cut this roll evenly into 1-inch sections. And guide with a ruler.

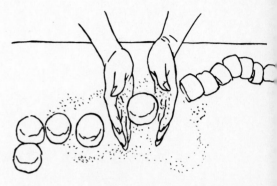

FIG. 4   Stand each of these sections on end and roll them between the palms of your hands into round cylinder.

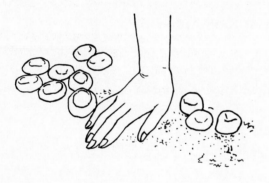

FIG. 5   Flatten these cylinders into round cakes.

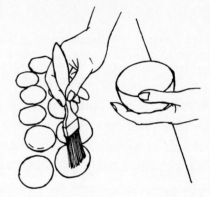

FIG. 6   Brush one side of each cake evenly with sesame seed oil or other vegetable oil.

204

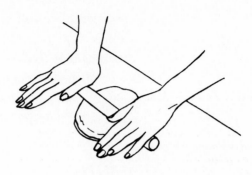

FIG. 7   Put one cake on top of another, oil sides together, and flatten the two cakes out smoothly with the heel of your hand.

FIG. 8   Now roll these pairs of cakes into flat thin pancakes. They must be rolled *firmly* and *evenly* to keep uniform thickness and the same size in each of the two cakes, about 7″ diameter.

To do this, rotate and turn over the pair of cakes frequently checking that the edges do not get too thick.

Pan fry each pair of the thin cakes, still together, in an ungreased skillet or griddle over medium low heat. The thin cakes should take less than one minute to get light brown spots on one side. Then turn to brown the other side for about ½ minute. The heat should be checked frequently so it does not get too high or too low. Pull the cooked cakes apart into two very thin cakes. Pile the thin cakes up and keep them covered to prevent their getting dried on the edges. Steam the thin cakes for about 10 minutes before serving to reheat them. (Do not let them touch the water while steaming.)

The pancakes may be placed on top of the rice while the rice is simmering, having aluminum foil between the rice and the cakes.

205

The easy way is to place a board close to frying pan and as you complete rolling, place pancake immediately into frying pan. While that is cooking prepare the next one. Pull them apart as soon as it is cooked.

If the pancakes are especially made for serving with Peking Duck, then make the dough into two even parts and proceed in the same manner. There will be 24 smaller pancakes instead of 12. The smaller pancakes should be 5″ in diameter.

EATING MANDARIN PANCAKES IN A PROPER WAY

Spread pancake out on clean plate. Put 2 or 3 TBS of filling, or 2 pieces of duck skin or meat in center.

Roll up as you would a cigarette.

Place roll in left hand supporting the ends on the thumb and small finger. Keep small finger raised slightly so as the oil or gravy if any, will stay in the roll and not drip. The right hand can remain free to use chopsticks or spoon on other dishes.

206

Menu Planning And Suggestions

 THE MAJORITY OF CHINESE HAVE HOT PORRIDGE
with several salty side dishes for breakfast. Some-
times pastries, sesame hot muffins and Chinese
doughnuts are also served. Most of them are easily
purchased from the little food stands at street corners. Most of the Chinese in this country enjoy the convenience
of serving the Americanized breakfast to their families.

Chinese families serve lunch same as dinner, having several
dishes together at the table — usually five or more. One soup is
in the center surrounded with four other dishes such as pork,
chicken, fish or shrimp (fresh or dried), which are cooked with
or without vegetables, and also there is an all-vegetable dish. Rich
families have more dishes at family meals, and when they enter-
tain friends the banquet is always served and cooked by their own
chefs or catered from restaurants. A banquet contains more than
ten dishes, sometimes twenty. First are cold plates which are
arranged artistically with many kinds of cold meats and vegetables, making a colorful array. Chinese warmed wine is served
at the same time, followed by four to six hot and delicate dishes.
The shelled shrimp dish is first to serve, then chicken, fish, etc.
These dishes are served one at a time. After the hot dishes comes
a clear and light soup. Then desserts (one, two or four, never
three) are served at this time, either sweet or salty pastries or
hot fruits. Now come four big heavy dishes such as whole ham,

207

duck, etc., decorated with some vegetables. Also there is a big bowl of soup with a whole chicken or duck in it, and rice is then served. When the dishes are almost at an end, usually there is no room for rice. This banquet lasts for a few hours, and with the wine-drinking games everybody is tired from eating so much and for so long. A cup of good hot tea is most desirable at this time.

Many poor Chinese families cannot afford to have meat very often, so it is needless for them to be concerned with flavor and texture. Old proverb: "Rich man's one banquet equals poor man's half year's food." 富人一夕酒，貧漢半年糧．

No matter, rich or poor, it is the tradition that we should not waste food. (Left-over banquet dishes are given to the servants.) We use almost every part of the ingredients which is edible. Of course there is no labor and time problem in China. All the children know they should eat every grain of rice in their bowls, otherwise they will marry somebody with a pockmarked face.

Planning your menu carefully and thoughtfully is a way to make your family life happier and your parties successful. There are a few important principles to follow for a good arrangement.

First of all, think of the balance of dishes you plan to serve. Do not repeat the same ingredients in too many dishes. For example, you may use mushrooms to prepare dishes, but I think to use them in two dishes is good enough; do not try to use them in all the dishes on the same table. To make your dishes appetizing, the balance of ingredients, of color, and of flavor is very important.

Do not serve only dishes which require last minute cooking. It will make you exhausted and unable to enjoy yourself in the happy gathering. I think one quick-stirring dish is enough, especially in more formal parties, where you have to spend time receiving your guests.

Food in season is cheaper and better. You can take advantage of it as fully as possible by using ingredients in season. There

208

might be an opened can of Chinese ingredients in your refrigerator; try to use it. When egg whites are used in a dish, you may save the yolks for other dishes such as Mandarin Eggs (see page 159). When you prepare a whole chicken by yourself, it is not necessary to use all those parts in a single day. You may keep some of them in your refrigerator or freezer and use them afterwards.

A good cook has the duty not only to present the best of food, but also to cover the weak points of ingredients. For example, the smell, which is the weak point of seafood, should be covered with some seasoning and spice.

When you are going to serve food to a party, think about the guests whom you will serve. What kind of food is liked or disliked by most of them? What are their respective religious backgrounds, and what is the degree of friendship between them and you or your family? Do not over-do for the party for your husband's boss. He will wonder where you get so much money. If you were born with a family fortune, sometimes it will also make his wife jealous. It is equally bad to do too little. It should be just right! Someone may be allergic to a certain food; try to avoid it or prepare another dish as substitute for this person. In summer serve more light and cold dishes; serve more heavy and hot dishes in winter. The majority of elderly persons prefer light food to heavy food. Jewish, Italian, and Far Eastern people like spicy and heavier dishes. Your attention to other people's dietary restrictions and your thoughtfulness will be greatly appreciated and rewarded richly.

Another advantage of Chinese cooking is economy. Many of the dishes only need a small amount of meat, and pork is always cheaper than other kinds of meat. This is very friendly to your pocket before the pay day.

Before you go to the market, I think it is definitely a good idea to put the names of the foods you want to buy on paper. That way you will not waste your energy going to the market for a second time.

It is advisable to list all dishes, even rice, you are going to serve and also put them in order. That is to say, which one should be cooked first and which one should be served first. Some of the dishes can be prepared earlier, or the day before, and may be half-cooked or reheated to serve. Also you may put some kinds of half-cooked dishes in the oven to complete the cooking or keep some of the cooked dishes warm in oven. Sometimes, when the dinner is about to be served, the hostess suddenly finds out the rice has not been cooked yet. In other cases, the whole dinner is about over, but there is still another dish in the refrigerator or in the oven. It is better to pin up the list of dishes in the kitchen and to check it frequently.

It is very hard for me to make each definite decision on what dishes are to be served together. This depends on the time, money, and the convenience of obtaining the ingredients. There is a rule in picking a menu so that the dishes will be balanced in flavor and appearance. For example, we never serve Shanghai Ham and Duck at the same time, or the Chicken with Mushrooms and Chicken Velvet together. Too many meat dishes are as bad as all vegetable dishes without meat.

I have listed all the dishes in the table of contents with different marks and suggestions so you make the choice to suit your situation. With the busy life here, of course, we could not cook as many dishes as in China. Also, usually, the family is not as big. So serve the dishes in the American way.

1 Appetizer
1 Soup
1 Main dish of poultry
or
beef
or

210

pork
or
seafood
or
egg

1 Vegetable — cooked or salad
Plain boiled or fried rice

When serving plain rice be sure the main dish is not too light such as Fried Shrimp (Chinese style), Mandarin Eggs, Cold Cut Chicken, Steamed Fish or Chicken Velvet which are all good for second main dish.

If two main dishes are used then do not choose both cooked by the quick-stirring method. Check the recipe for the way of cooking.

If you want to serve a third main dish then select something that can be served cold or use two vegetables — one cooked and one salad.

For serving to a large party do not use heavily spiced dishes because not everyone likes hot flavored dishes — unless you know they love it.

To people who claim they do not like Chinese food, or if the Chinese food is new to them, then serve dishes cooked without soy sauce and not heavily spiced. Many times I have tried beef with vegetable dishes on this sort of guest and have had good results.

Some dishes are welcomed by most children. When you serve children, especially the younger ones at birthday parties, it is better to have all the food on the same plate without soup. For example, few slices pork strips, one big scoopful main dish, and one large scoopful of fried rice. Children always like fried rice better than plain boiled. (In your family it will be easy to find out what dishes are suited to them as everybody's taste is different.)

In the index you will find some appetizers noted as being good hors d'oeuvres. Also a list of dishes good for midnight snacks with close friends.

Since many of the dishes are so authentic, it will be fun to eat in an authentic way and will be especially interesting to the Chinese guests or those people who have been in China before. The following dishes are especially good for this sort of guest.

Hot and Sour Peking soup or Chinese Celery Cabbage soup

Mandarin Moo Shi pork with pancakes

(If for a large party, increase the amount of above dishes or add another dish of)

Pork with Bean Thread

Crabmeat with eggs

Spinach, Chinese style (If it is to be wrapped with pancake, then drain off liquid after cooking)

Peking Meat Sauce Noodles (For whole meal)

Peking duck

Chinese Celery Cabbage soup

Mandarin eggs

Pork with Bean Sprouts

Peking Duck is very good to serve first as an appetizer. If you serve plain boiled rice with Peking Duck, then a heavy dish with gravy and a vegetable should be served.

Fried rice, wonton soup or noodles are good for a simple lunch. It would be nice with a vegetable salad.

Seasoned Black Mushrooms, Jellied Lamb Loaf, and Sweet and Sour Cabbage relish are very good for side dishes.

Almond Float and Pea Jelly Square are good to serve at a large party. Almost everybody likes Almond Float especially.

Almond Tea and Steamed Egg Cake should not be served after a heavy meal. They are better for afternoon.

Orange Tapioca is good in cold weather.

Serve noodles at birthday parties to assure long life for the honored guest.

212

Tips In Shopping For Food

An old chinese proverb: no matter how capable a wife is, she cannot cook rice without rice. 巧婦難為無米之炊.

Cooked rice and raw rice have different characters in Chinese. Good dishes depend on good ingredients — the right kind and fresh. So shopping for food is certainly as important as cooking it.

CHICKEN

A fresh chicken has a better, tastier flavor and a good aroma. (In all kinds of meat, the fresher they are, the less undesirable the odor they have.) Buying a live chicken is a definite way of getting it fresh but there are only a few places which sell it that way in a big city. If you happen to know such a place, do buy there even though it means more work. You will be rewarded later with delicious dishes. If you live in the country you probably have enjoyed the good taste of freshly killed chicken.

When you buy chicken from the super market, you will have the convenience of picking the exact part which the recipe calls for. If it is not wrapped, choose the skin of the bird which is dry and clean, not sticky, and the meat is translucent and odorless. If it is packed in cellophane, rub the wrapper against the chicken skin to test stickiness. In buying frozen chicken check the back to see if it has a heavy, reddish or bloody ice-coating. This would

213

mean that the bird had not been quick-frozen or it had been defrosted before.

Be sure to check the recipe you are going to make, to select the right kind of chicken or the right chicken parts.

DUCK Frozen duckling is very handy to use and easy to clean. The fresh duck is larger and has a heavier skin, good for making Peking Duck. Because of the amount of work involved in the pulling of feathers, I suggest you use the frozen duckling — unless, of course, your family volunteers to help you.

Select frozen duckling as you would frozen chicken. Look for clean smooth skin without bloody frost in the package.

BEEF Always try to buy flank steak for sliced or shredded beef in recipes. It is not only less expensive, but also easy to cut, as the grain lies in one direction. A cut called "skirt" steak is also reasonably priced. Sirloin and top rump are good but cost much more. The best choice is meat with good red color, firm and little fat.

PORK When you buy pork, it is better to pick meat that is firm, with a bright deep pink and white fat. For economy always choose the leaner cuts. Pick shoulder and fresh ham with clean smooth skin. Test the freshness of a large piece of meat by punching it with your finger tip. If the meat springs back, it is fresh. *Spare Ribs*: If you prefer tender spare ribs, choose the pieces that have shorter rib bones. They are from smaller pigs.

SHRIMP I have never seen fresh shrimp in New England, only frozen. If you are lucky enough to live where you can get live,

214

fresh shrimp, you can enjoy its smooth juicy meat.

Frozen shrimp when firm, blueish in color, and translucent are better. Florida shrimp are pink and not very shiny, but always make sure they are firm. To be sure the shrimp is fresh ask the clerk to defrost some especially for you, even if you must pay a little more. If you have room in your freezer it is better to buy a 5-lb. frozen package and defrost the shrimp as needed. Buy medium or small size as the recipes in this book do not need the more expensive large or jumbo size. Do not buy cooked shrimp for Chinese dishes. Even in your American dishes I think they are over-cooked and dry.

Recently, frozen shrimp, shelled, deveined, and packed in plastic bags, has become available in large super markets. Another kind of tiny shrimp, frozen in blocks, is available at seafood whole-sale suppliers. Both of them are suitable for Chinese cooking. All frozen shrimps should be defrosted for Chinese cooking, even when package is marked "not necessary to defrost."

LOBSTER

Buy only live lobsters with old shells — or called hard shell. If you must buy them at the super market, choose the heavy active ones.

In New England the better way is to buy lobsters from a wholesaler who keeps them alive in big salt-water tanks. Look in the yellow pages of the telephone book to find such dealers, and probably it is wise to phone them before you go. In special and fancy fish markets you can also get good lobsters.

FISH

Choose fish as you would meat. Fresh fish meat is firm, shiny and translucent, and you will find little or no water in the tray where it is on display. When buying whole fish, see that it has bulging, shiny eyes, bright red gills, and shiny, clean scales or skin.

215

I still remember that once when I was about 12 years old, my mother asked me to pick up some fresh-water fish from a friendly fish dealer on my way home from school. In China, the fresh-water fish are always kept alive in open large wooden basins. I had heard how to judge fresh fish and to check the gills. I insisted on looking at the gills to see whether they were red or not. Since you cannot do this except on a dead fish, for a long time this was a joke between the dealer and my family.

VEGETABLES   Regular cabbage — In Chinese cooking I like to use new cabbage rather than old. The tight-leaved, heavy, egg-shaped ones are tender and crisp.

Chinese celery cabbage — The firm, heavy, tight-leaved white ones are better.

Broccoli — Fresh broccoli has flower buds that are all green and tight with no dry or brown stalks.

Radish — Radishes are sold by the bunch; judge them by the green tops. If the leaves are quite dry or rotten, the radishes are not fresh and will be hollow and limp. To test hollowness, press the radish between the thumb and index finger. Hollow radishes are soft. A fresh radish has a smooth and bright red skin, and if it is egg-shaped then it is more crisp. Radishes with a rough skin are tough and contain worms. Sometimes they even have little worm holes on the skin. Radishes packed in plastic bags, even if washed, still need trimming. Normally they are stored longer and therefore are not very sweet and crisp.

Cucumber — Narrow, small cucumbers are tender and crisp, and are good for Mandarin Cucumber Soup (page 87) and salads. Greenhouse cucumber is big but is also crisp. For making Stuffed Cucumber (page 138) choose the cucumbers which are thick and straight. Sometimes cucumbers are waxed for more protection in winter. If so, the skin should be removed before cooking or making salad.

Asparagus — the greener the asparagus, the more tender and the less waste. Do not buy asparagus with dry tips; that shows the vegetable has been kept for many days.

Spinach — Spinach leaves which are firm and green are good. If you buy plastic-packed spinach be sure no rotten leaves show inside the bag. Fresh, loose spinach (use the stalks also) is delicious, even though it means more washing. Frozen spinach is not suitable to use in Chinese cooking, as it is already over-cooked.

Green beans — Cooked fresh-picked green beans are tender and delicious. If you buy beans at the super market check the freshness by seeing that the tips are not brown and they are not wrinkled. Frozen green beans may be used in Chinese cooking.

Green peas — Frozen green peas are suitable for Chinese cooking. Canned peas are too soft and not green enough.

To be on the safe side, when you pick out the dishes for your meal, especially for a party, it is better to have a second choice; if you are not able to obtain the ingredients for the first one you can rely on your second selection.

Almost all Chinese groceries and noodle factories are located in so-called Chinatowns. There are many of them in these areas. When shopping you can walk along and try any of them with the Chinese ingredients shopping list found in the rear of this book. Some of the owners do not speak English fluently but they understand the Chinese characters on the list.

The groceries and noodle factories listed are friendly and carry the ingredients called for in this book. I list them here and in return they will be kind and patient with you. If you have any comments, I will be very interested to know.

Sunday is an exciting day to shop in Chinatown. Store-keepers will display more ingredients and some of the stores also have roasted and cooked meat, ducks and chickens. Chinese laundry owners do their shopping on Sunday. Another convenience of Sunday shopping is parking. Try to be there before noon as it will not be too crowded and the storekeepers will give you more attention. Some Japanese groceries also handle Chinese ingredients.

JOYCE CHEN ASSOCIATES
MAIL ORDER DEPARTMENT

The inconvenience of getting Chinese ingredients limits many people from cooking Chinese dishes. I feel it is not only necessary to offer you the right recipes, but also the right ingredients to make your Chinese cooking successful.

The Joyce Chen mail order department is conducted directly by me, offering you the best Chinese ingredients packed in convenient quantities. It operates in a friendly and secure way.

Write to Joyce Chen, P. O. Box 3, Cambridge, Massachusetts 02138, for more information.

Important Information
In Chinese Cooking

To MAKE YOUR CHINESE COOKING SUCCESSFUL and easier, the following information is important:

Be sure to read this whole book first before choosing a recipe.

Read recipes thoroughly before shopping for and readying the ingredients.

Read at least once more before starting to prepare and cook.

When you cook food in quick-stirring method it is very necessary to prepare every ingredient first and line them up within reaching distance. A small bowl of water or the water kettle should be nearby in case the food gets dry or starts to burn. Add a little water or lift the skillet off heat until everything is under control.

As I have said before, the first item which is put into the skillet with hot oil should be as dry as possible, because oil will spatter more when anything wet is added. It is a very big noise when the first ingredient is added to the hot oil, so be sure to warn the people who are in the kitchen and keep the children away from the stove.

Simmering food with heavy liquids should be checked often, or leave the cover open a little so in case the heat is too high the liquid will not overflow.

219

When reheating left-overs in sauce pan or skillet, a little water (about 2-4 TBS) should be added to avoid burning and replace the water which evaporates.

The easy way to skim fat off liquid in such dishes as Shanghai duck and ham, etc., is to remove the cold, firm fat which has settled on it in storing, and then reheat.

For stirring and turning soft ingredients, use the back of spoon or wooden spoon in pushing motion while rotating the pan sharply for less breakage.

In cutting soft, spongy, or outside crisp and inside soft articles, it is better to use sawing motion with a sharp knife for neat and uncrushed edges.

Cut onions under or in front of an exhaust fan to prevent eyes from tearing.

Corn starch is very easy to mix with water but it always sets on the bottom of bowl, so be sure to stir well before *quickly* mixing with hot liquids.

Sometimes the lowest heat or flame is still too high for low simmering, such as for simmering chicken broth, etc. Move the pan half off the heat, stirring the ingredients occasionally for even tenderness.

Left-over oil from deep frying may be strained through a very fine strainer and used again. Do *not* re-use the oil which is used for frying fish without batter such as Soy Sauce fish, Shanghai style.

Always use more than enough water in cooking, parboiling or soaking ingredients in which the water will be discarded later.

Sometimes there are a few dark spots in the raw rice. It is better to discard these before cooking; check them while washing.

Store brown sugar in a plastic bag to avoid hardening. If leftover sugar has hardened transfer it to a small plastic bag. After a few days the lumps can then be more easily loosened and softened by rubbing the bag with your finger tips.

Words From The Author

When writing this book I often told my daughter, Helen, that it was written with blood, sweat and love. Blood and sweat for the hard work in testing, researching, and struggling with my poor English. All the recipes have been used not only in my cooking classes but also been tested several times before putting into this book to ensure successful results. Love to both my old and new countries in preserving the authentic flavors and the ways of cooking; love in remembering the old days in China where I was born, grew up and lived for more than thirty years; love to my new country for the freedom, wonderful friendships and good opportunities which my family and I have enjoyed since we came here. I worked my best to simplify the procedures for the busy American life, giving enough information to lead the beginner to the enjoyment of cooking, serving and eating those dishes from the other side of the world which they have never seen.

In addition, I wish to have my fellow Chinese and the people who have been in China have the dishes which they have missed for a long time.

Most of all, my deep appreciation to these people who have helped me make this book available to you at its best:

Mr. John Brook	Mr. Wei-ling Liao
Mrs. Nicolas Bloembergen	Mr. Donald Outerbridge
Mrs. Samuel Caldwell	Mr. Paul R. Rugo
Mr. William Cavness	Mrs. Thomas Rodgers
Mr. Te-cheng Chiang	Miss Pamela Smith
Mr. Lewis Clark	Mr. and Mrs. Walter Tower Jr.
Mr. H. Vose Greenough, Jr.	Dr. and Mrs. Paul Dudley White
Prof. and Mrs. Rolf Haugen	Prof. Robert S. Woodbury
Prof. Ming-chich Ho	Mr. and Mrs. Thomas Wilson
Prof. and Mrs. Howard Mumford Jones	Prof. and Mrs. Lien-sheng Yang
Mrs. William Kinter	Mr. Richard Young
Prof. and Mrs. Y. W. Lee	Mr. Zunvair John Yue

Also, I received much encouragement from friends, members of my cooking classes, customers at the restaurant, and my family, especially my youngest son, Stephen.

Cooking is an art — an unselfish art which you will enjoy sharing with others. From the bottom of my heart I wish you will enjoy this book. God bless you, the unselfish artist.

Shopping List

CHINESE NAME	ENGLISH NAME	REMARKS
竹筍	Bamboo shoots	In can from Taiwan and Japan
豆腐	Bean curd	In small cakes or large pad
醬	Bean paste	In 1 lb. can or Japanese miso by lb.
豆芽	Bean sprouts	Buy fresh or grow at home
粉絲	Bean thread	In 2, 4, or 8 oz. cellophane pkgs.
豆豉	Salted black beans	In plastic bag
冬菇	Black mushrooms	Sold dry by weight, ¼ to 1 lb.
珠油	Brown gravy syrup	In jars or from super market
白菜	Chinese cabbage	Firm, shorter and unflowered is better
火腿	Chinese ham (Smithfield)	Buy from Chinese grocery in slices by lb., or whole
川椒 (花椒)	Chinese pepper corn	If not available in grocery, try Chinese drug store
蘇梅醬	Duck sauce	Domestic gallon jar or imported in can
春捲皮	Egg roll skin	Chinese noodle factory (and some groceries) by lb., thinner skins are better.
薑	Ginger	Smooth skin and large piece is better
金針	Golden needle	In 1 lb. block, light color is better

Shopping List

CHINESE NAME	ENGLISH NAME	REMARKS
海鮮醬	Hoi Sin sauce	In square or round cans. Round is easier to open
味粉	Monosodium glutamate powder	1 lb. pkg. from Chinese grocery is much cheaper
芥末	Mustard	By weight. ¼ lb. is enough
麵	Noodles	Dried or fresh from Chinese noodle factory or super market
蠔油	Oyster sauce	In bottle. Imported is better
麻油	Sesame oil	Small 6 oz. bottle is suitable
蝦米	Shrimp, dried	By weight. ¼ lb. is enough.
雪豆	Snow peas	By weight. Price changes daily.
醬油	Soy sauce	Japanese-made good for dipping
五香粉	Spice powder	In 1 lb. bag (or smaller, if available)
大茴香	Star anise	1 or 2 oz. will last long time
馬蹄 (荸薺)	Water chestnuts	Buy from Chinese grocery, is fresher
冬瓜	Winter melon	In slices, by weight
雲耳 (木耳)	Wood ear (Black Fungus)	Light in weight. Few oz. will last a long time